For Apple II, II+ IIe & IIc

Apple Graphics

Low-Res programs and activities.

Bob Hofemann

ENRICH/OHAUS
San Jose, California 95131

Graphic Design by Kaye Graphics
Cover and Poster Illustration by Kaye Quinn
Illustrations by Corb Hillam

Editorial Direction by Contemporary Ideas, Inc.
Edited by Jim Haugaard

Typography by KGN Graphics

Published by
ENRICH/OHAUS
2325 Paragon Drive
San Jose, CA 95131
U.S.A.

For information on rights and distribution outside the U.S.A., please write ENRICH/OHAUS at the above address.

ISBN: 0-86582-165-8
Catalog No. EN79251
Printed in the United States of America
10 9 8 7 6 5 4 3 2 1

Table of Contents

INTRODUCTION TO GRAPHICS 5
Use of GR, COLOR =, and PLOT in Low-Resolution graphics.

DRAWING HORIZONTAL LINES 11
Use of HLIN statements in graphics.

DRAWING VERTICAL LINES 15
Use of VLIN statements in graphics.

FOR-NEXT LOOPS AND GRAPHICS 19
Use of FOR-NEXT loops and variables.

DIAGONAL PLOTS 27
Use of FOR-NEXT loops.

FLASH 29
Use of FOR-NEXT loops and random numbers.

GRAPHICS ANIMATION 33
Use of FOR-NEXT loops, subroutines.

READ/DATA IN GRAPHICS 37
Use of READ/DATA statements.

GRAPHICS LETTERS AND NUMBERS 43
Examples of graphics letters and numbers.

GRAPH PAPER PAGE 44
Blank Low-Resolution graph paper page.

ANSWER KEY TO SELECTED PROBLEMS 45
Answers to selected Computer Challenges.

GLOSSARY OF TERMS 48
Definition of computer terms.

Introduction

Using a computer to draw graphics pictures is fun! This book is designed to give you the necessary commands and programming knowledge to draw video pictures and make them move on the screen.

This book will take you step-by-step through beginning graphics commands. Each chapter includes detailed directions and exercises to help you learn graphics programming. Easy to understand exercises lead you through each chapter. Computer challenges following each chapter give you a chance to try out the skills you have learned. Part of the fun in creating graphics is to change an existing program. As you work through this book, experiment and change the program lines to get a result that you want.

You will need many sheets of blank low-resolution graph paper to construct your drawings. Only one blank sheet (see page 44) is provided in this book. You will have to make copies of this page to effectively use this book.

Apple Graphics includes beginning and intermediate graphics statements in low-resolution graphics available in Applesoft BASIC. You will learn to use FOR-NEXT loops and READ/DATA statements to animate graphics figures. A graphics page is included with examples of graphics letters and numbers. An answer key to selected problems in Computer Challenges is included to help you if you need it.

The programs in this book are written in Applesoft BASIC for the Apple II Plus and Apple IIe computers. The programs will run on monochrome or color monitors. The COLOR statements in the programs will appear in different shades of monochrome if you do not have a color monitor.

Experimenting with computer graphics is exciting. Creating graphics pictures and animating them will give you many hours of enjoyment. Have fun!

Introduction to Graphics

Drawing pictures with computer graphics is fun. The Apple computer has two kinds of graphics: (1) low-resolution and (2) high-resolution. They are usually called "lo-res" and "hi-res" graphics. This book is about low-resolution graphics.

Low-resolution drawings are made by lighting up small cells of color on the screen. The cells are shaped like rectangles. They are only about half as high as they are wide.

In low-res graphics, the screen can display 40 cells vertically (up and down). It can display 40 cells horizontally (side to side).

Four lines are reserved for text at the bottom of the screen.

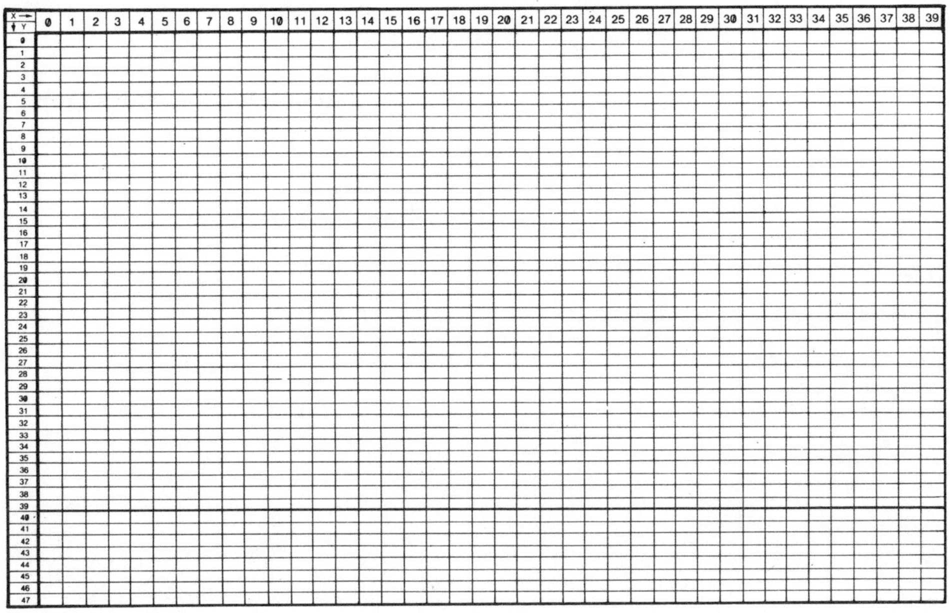

The drawings in this book will be displayed in color if you have a color monitor or t.v. They will also work if your screen display has only two colors.

The Apple computer has special commands for drawing graphics pictures. If you want to draw pictures, you have to type in a command that tells the computer to display graphics.

`GR` (Tells the computer to change the screen to display low-resolution graphics)

Look at the grid below. It represents the upper-left corner of your display screen.

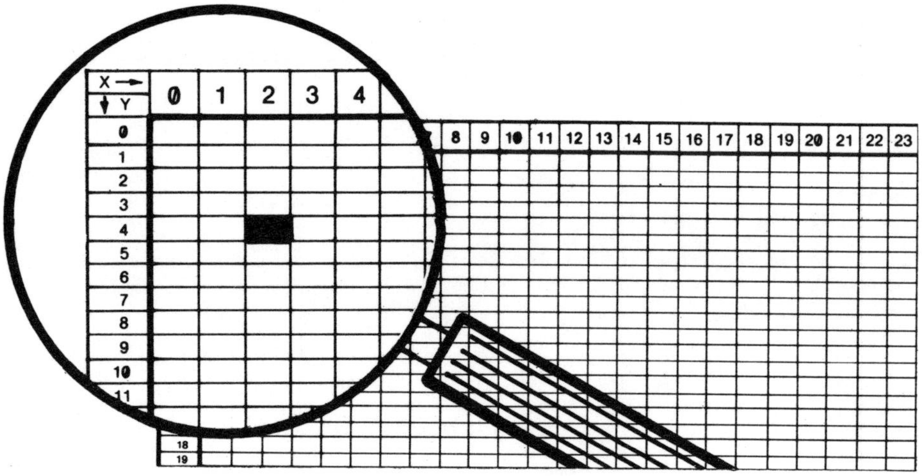

Each cell or rectangle has a location on the video screen. The location of the cell that is shown is 2,4. (Two cells to the right of 0,0 and four cells down.)

To light up the rectangle on your screen, you need two other graphics commands. They are `COLOR =` and `PLOT`

```
GR
```

`COLOR = 15` (Tells the computer the color to use is white.)

`PLOT 2,4` (Tells the computer the location of the rectangle on the screen.)

TRY THIS:

Type in the three commands.

Press the <RETURN> key after each one.

Your monitor or t.v. screen should look like this:

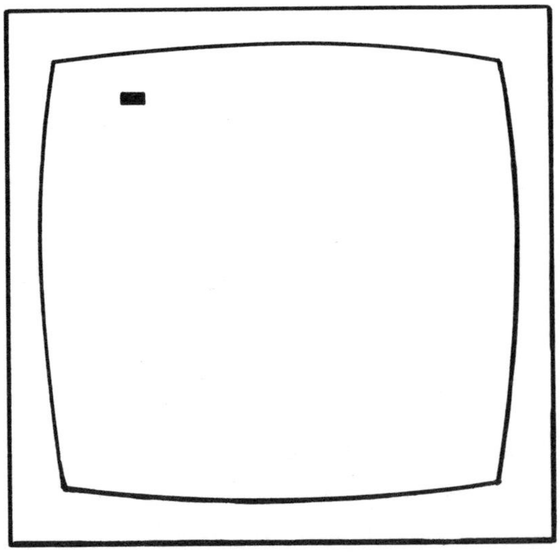

Adding Line Numbers

Line numbers are used in graphics programs. The computer stores programs with line numbers in its memory. These programs can be run again and again.

When line numbers are placed in front of computer instructions, the computer begins with the smallest line number and continues to the next larger line number.

THE COMPUTER COUNTS CELLS TO THE RIGHT AND THEN DOWN.

Look at the program below:

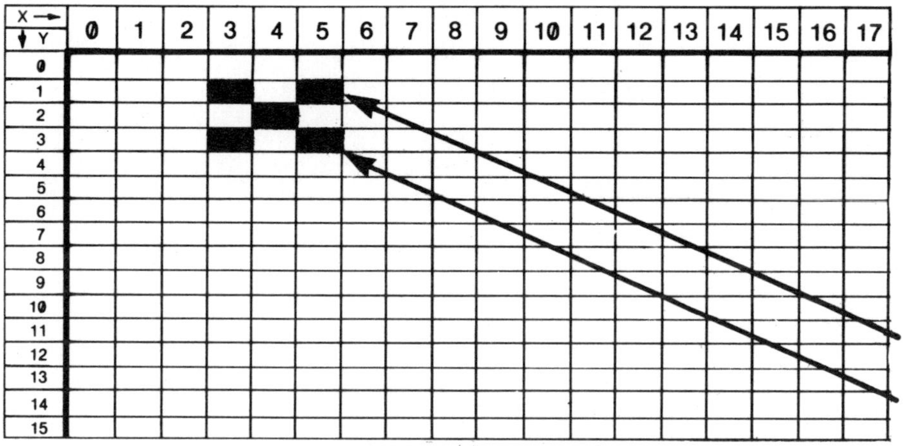


```
10 GR
20 COLOR = 15
30 PLOT 3, 1
40 PLOT 3, 3
50 PLOT 4, 2
60 PLOT 5, 1
70 PLOT 5, 3
```

Each Plot Statement LIGHTS UP A CELL ON THE DISPLAY

TRY THIS:

Type in the program

Type in RUN and press RETURN — (The command RUN tells the computer to follow the instructions in your program)

Type in TEXT and press RETURN — (TEXT changes the screen display from the graphics to text characters)

Using the TEXT and NEW commands

When you RUN a graphics program the screen display is changed for graphics. If you want the normal text screen back, you must type TEXT and press the <RETURN> key. The screen will change to text characters. To completely clear the screen, you must type TEXT and press the <RETURN> key and then type HOME and press the <RETURN> key. Try it.

If you type LIST, your program will be listed on the display screen. If you do not type TEXT first, you will only see text in the bottom four lines on the graphics screen.

The command NEW erases the current program from the computer's memory. Before you type in a new program, you should type the word NEW and press the return key.

What if I Make a Mistake?

If the computer gives you an error message such as ?SYNTAX ERROR, follow these steps:

(1) Type in TEXT and press the <RETURN> key.
(This command "turns off" the graphics display)

(2) Type in LIST and press the <RETURN> key.
(This command tells the computer to list your program)

(3) Look at each line number and the words or symbols after it. Your program lines must be exactly like the ones shown in the program.

(4) When you find the line with an error, type in the line number and the commands again. Then press the <RETURN> key.

(5) Type in LIST and press the <RETURN> key to see if the line is correct.

(6) Type in RUN and the computer will follow the instructions in your program.

Colors in low-res graphics

The apple computer can display the following colors:

0	BLACK	6	MEDIUM BLUE	11	PINK
1	RED	7	LIGHT BLUE	12	LIGHT GREEN
2	DARK BLUE	8	BROWN	13	YELLOW
3	PURPLE	9	ORANGE	14	AQUA (BLUE-GREEN)
4	DARK GREEN	10	GRAY	15	WHITE
5	GRAY				

NOTE: If you do not have a monitor that displays colors, they will appear in shades of gray.

TRY THIS:

Type in this program and RUN it.

Change line number 20 by retyping it.
Change COLOR = 15 to another color from 0 through 15. For example: 20 COLOR = 7.
RUN the program again.

Then, type NEW and press <RETURN>.

```
NEW
10 GR
20 COLOR = 15
30 PLOT 3,1
40 PLOT 3,3
50 PLOT 4,2
60 PLOT 5,1
70 PLOT 5,3
```

(1) Write a program that will place a cell of color in each corner of your display screen.
For Example:

```
10 GR

20 COLOR = 15

30

40

50

60

70 END
```

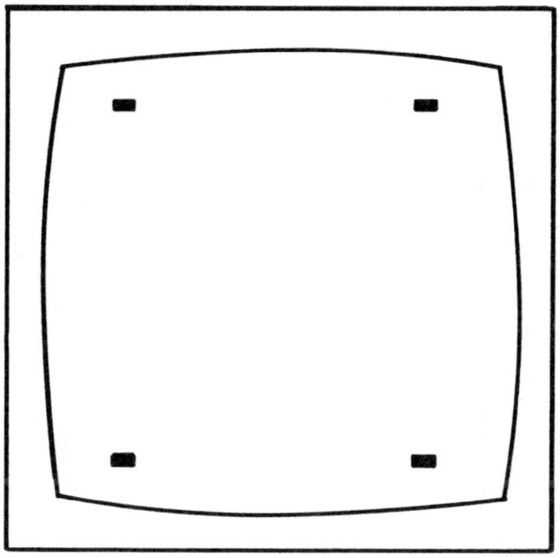

(2) Type NEW and press <RETURN>. Write the missing line numbers in the program to draw a red arrow. The line numbers below show which cells are already plotted.

```
10

20

30 PLOT 14,4

40 PLOT 15,4

50 PLOT 16,4

60 PLOT 17,4

70 PLOT 18,4

80

90

100

110

120 END
```

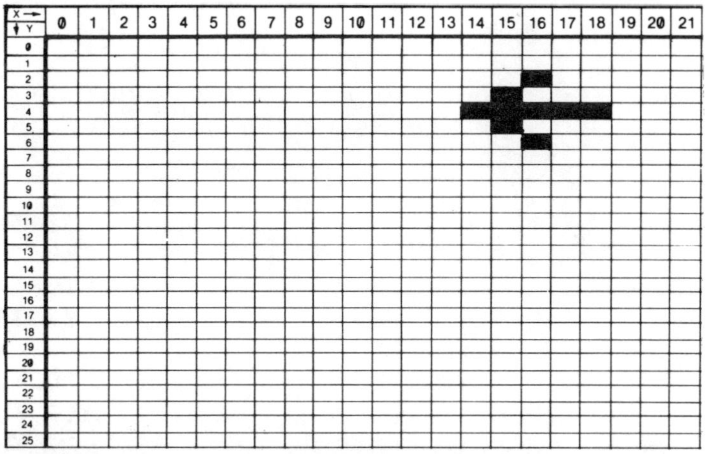

(3) Type NEW and press <RETURN>. Write the PLOT statements that will turn the frown into a smile. Use the program below as an example.

```
10 GR

20 COLOR = 15

30 PLOT 17,24

40 PLOT 21,24

50 PLOT 19,26

60 PLOT 18,30

70 PLOT 19,30

80 PLOT 20,30

90

100

110 END
```

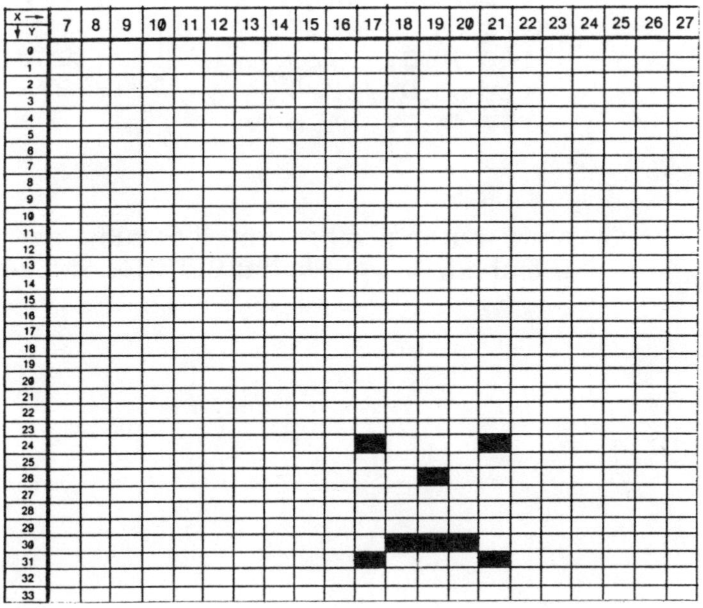

Computer Challenges

(1) Write the program that PLOTS the circle shown below.

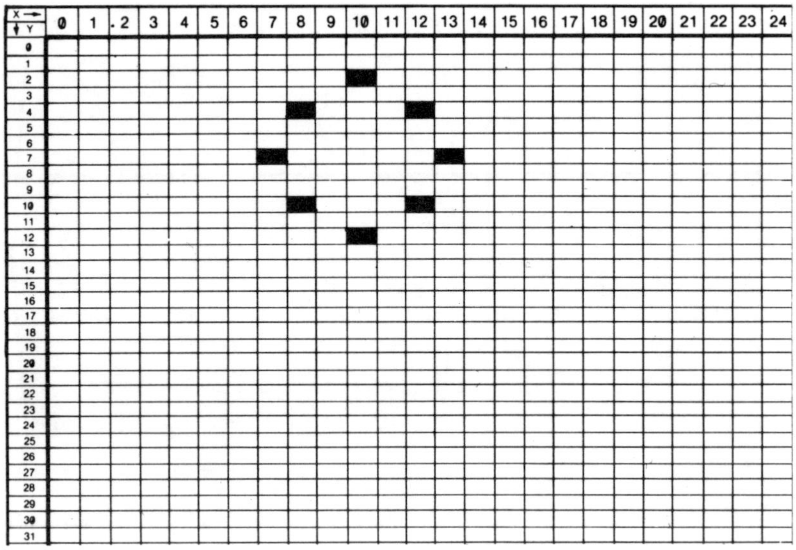

(2) You are going to play the role of the computer. Using a low-resolution graph sheet (see p. 44) and a pencil, shade in the PLOT commands in the program below and draw the figure.

```
10 GR
20 COLOR = 15
30 PLOT 10,5
40 PLOT 12,5
50 PLOT 15,5
60 PLOT 17,5
70 PLOT 11,6
80 PLOT 16,6
90 PLOT 10,7
100 PLOT 12,7
110 PLOT 15,7
120 PLOT 17,7
130 PLOT 13,8
140 PLOT 14,8
150 PLOT 13,9
160 PLOT 14,9
170 PLOT 10,10
180 PLOT 12,10
190 PLOT 15,10
200 PLOT 17,10
210 PLOT 11,11
220 PLOT 16,11
230 PLOT 10,12
240 PLOT 12,12
250 PLOT 15,12
260 PLOT 17,12
270 END
```

(3) Write a graphics program that will draw your first initial. Use a low-resolution graphics sheet and shade in your initial BEFORE you write the program.

Drawing Horizontal Lines

Using PLOT statements to draw a picture takes a lot of typing. The Apple computer can draw lines as well as PLOT cells. You can draw horizontal (side to side) lines on your display screen. Look at the grid below.

This program draws a blue horizontal line:

```
10 GR
20 COLOR = 7
30 HLIN 5,20 AT 5
```

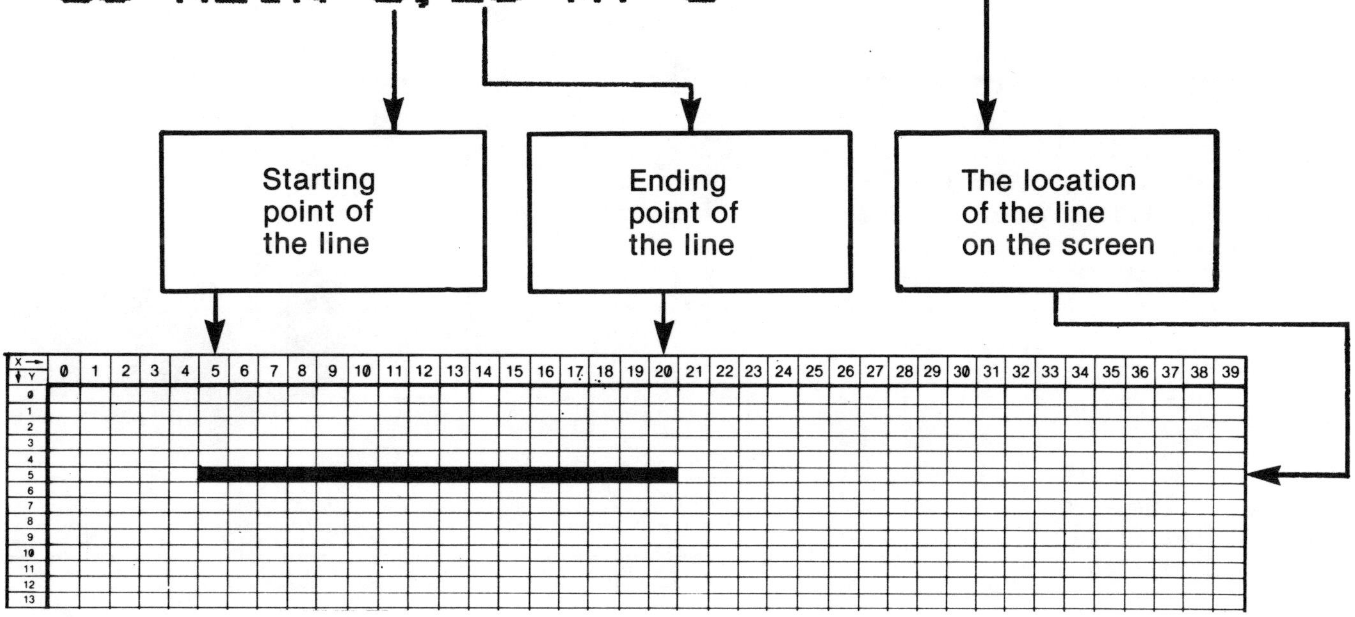

This program draws a green horizontal line:

```
10 GR
20 COLOR = 4
30 HLIN 3,12 AT 7
```

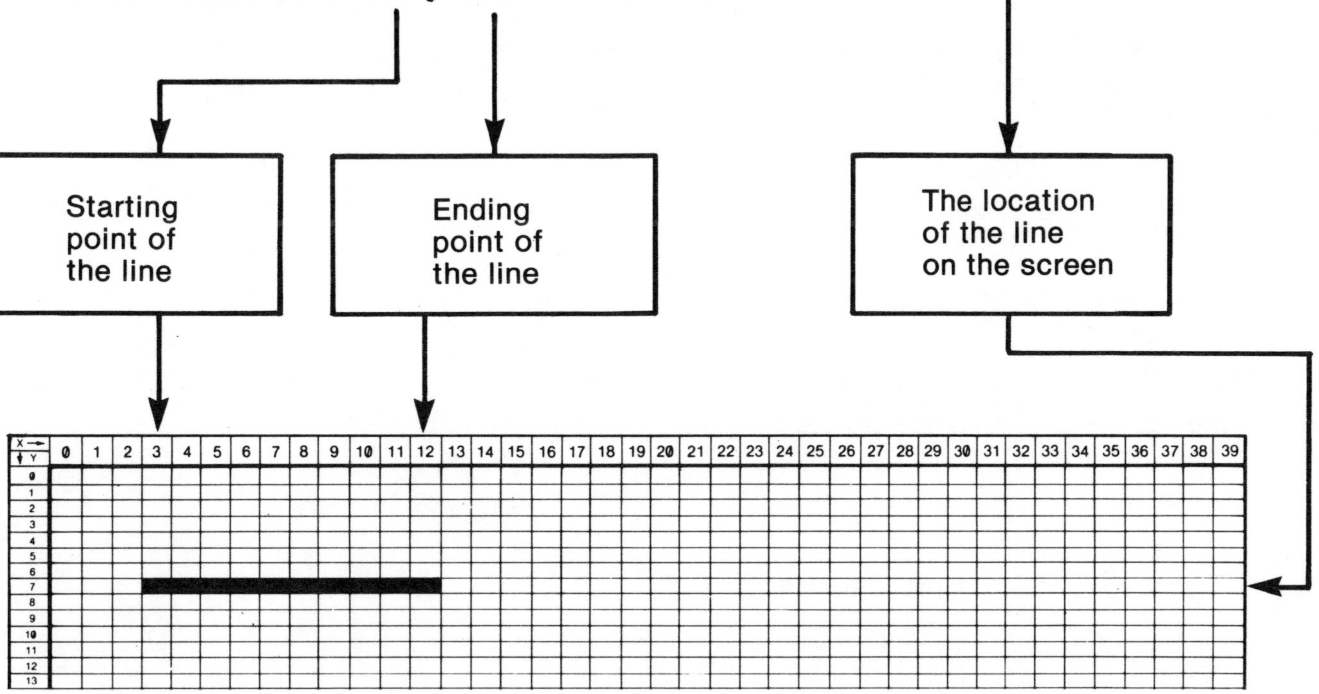

TRY THIS:

Look at the program and the figure that is drawn on the right. Each line number with a HLIN statement draws one of the horizontal lines. Type is this program and RUN it.

```
10 GR
20 COLOR = 6
30 PLOT 14,20
40 PLOT 20,20
50 HLIN 13,15 AT 21
60 HLIN 19,21 AT 21
70 HLIN 12,16 AT 22
80 HLIN 18,22 AT 22
90 HLIN 12,22 AT 23
100 HLIN 11,23 AT 24
110 HLIN 11,23 AT 25
120 HLIN 11,23 AT 26
130 HLIN 12,22 AT 27
140 HLIN 12,22 AT 28
150 HLIN 13,21 AT 29
160 HLIN 14,20 AT 30
170 HLIN 15,19 AT 31
180 HLIN 16,18 AT 32
190 PLOT 17,33
200 END
```

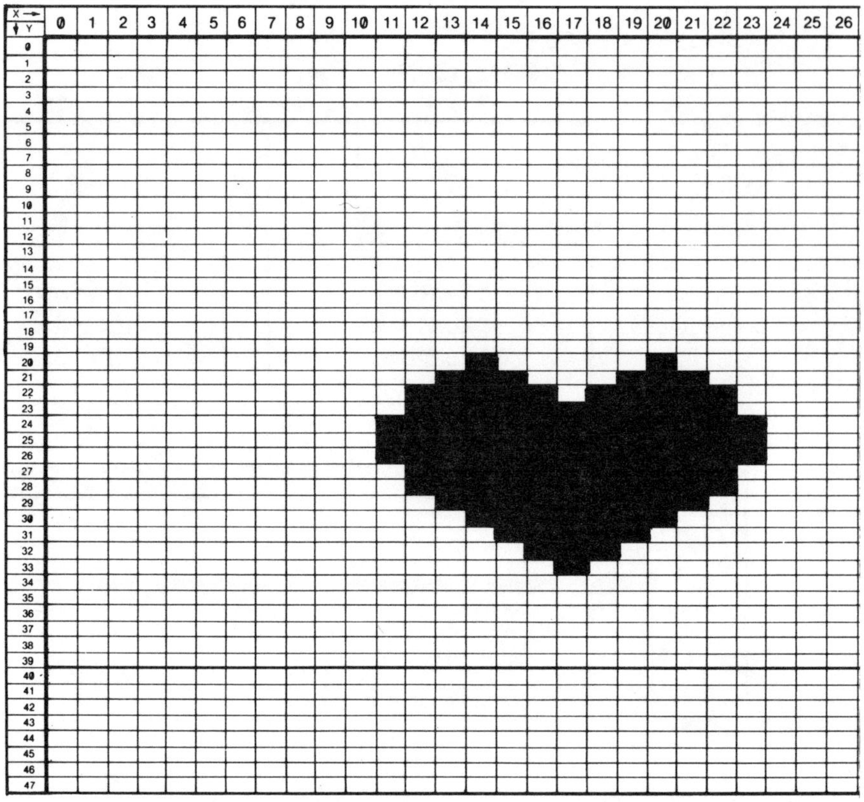

More than one statement on a line

You can type more than one graphics command on a single line in a program. If you place more than one command on a line, the commands must be separated by a colon (:).

TRY THIS:

Type in the program line numbers shown below:

```
10 GR
20 COLOR = 15
30 PLOT 17,5:PLOT 18:6
40 PLOT 21,6:PLOT 22,5
50 HLIN 19,20 AT 7
```

Don't type NEW. There is more to follow.

Type in TEXT.

Type LIST and add the following lines to your program:

```
60 HLIN 18,21 AT 8
70 HLIN 17,22 AT 9
80 HLIN 19,20 AT 10
90 PLOT 17,10:PLOT 22,10
100 HLIN 16,23 AT 11
110 HLIN 15,16 AT 12
120 HLIN 23,24 AT 12
130 PLOT 18,12:PLOT 21,12
140 END
RUN
```

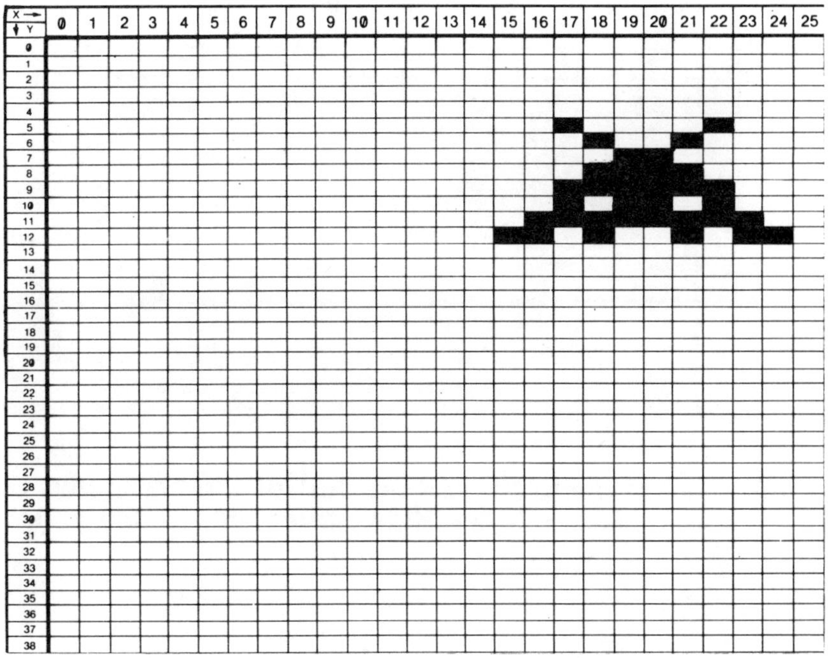

Your screen display should look like the ALIEN INVADER shown above.

TRY THIS:

Type in TEXT.

Type LIST.

Add line numbers to your program that will fill in the missing parts of the drawing shown on the right. The missing parts are marked with X's. Use PLOT and HLIN statements. Don't foget to add an END statement.

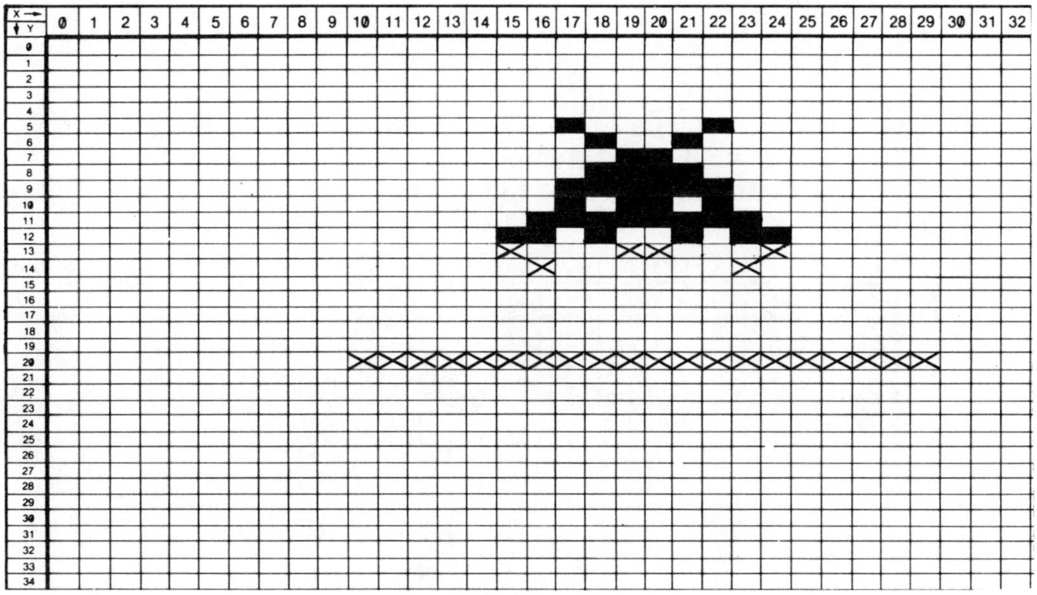

(1) Using HLIN and PLOT statements, write a program that draws this tree.

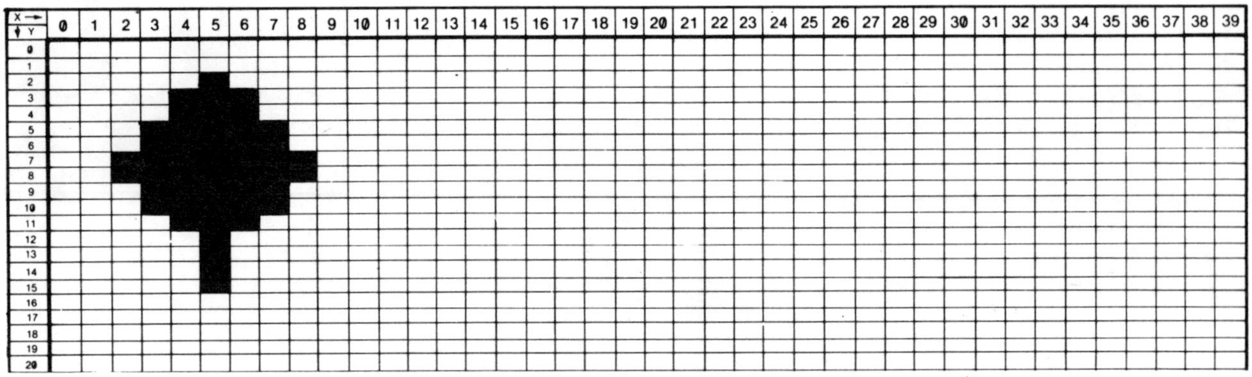

(2) You are going to play the part of the computer. Use a low-resolution graph sheet as your screen. Shade in the HLIN statements with a pencil and draw the figure.

```
10 GR
20 COLOR = 15
30 HLIN 8,10 AT 4
40 HLIN 6,12 AT 5
50 HLIN 15,17 AT 5
60 HLIN 5,13 AT 6
70 HLIN 15,17 AT 6
80 HLIN 4,17 AT 7
90 HLIN 3,15 AT 8
100 HLIN 4,14 AT 9
110 HLIN 5,13 AT 10
120 HLIN 6,7 AT 11
130 HLIN 11,12 AT 11
140 HLIN 6,7 AT 12
150 HLIN 11,12 AT 12
```

(3) Use a separate piece of paper to write a graphics program that draws the Apple. Use HLIN, PLOT and COLOR = statements in your program so the display looks like the multi-colored APPLE TRADEMARK.

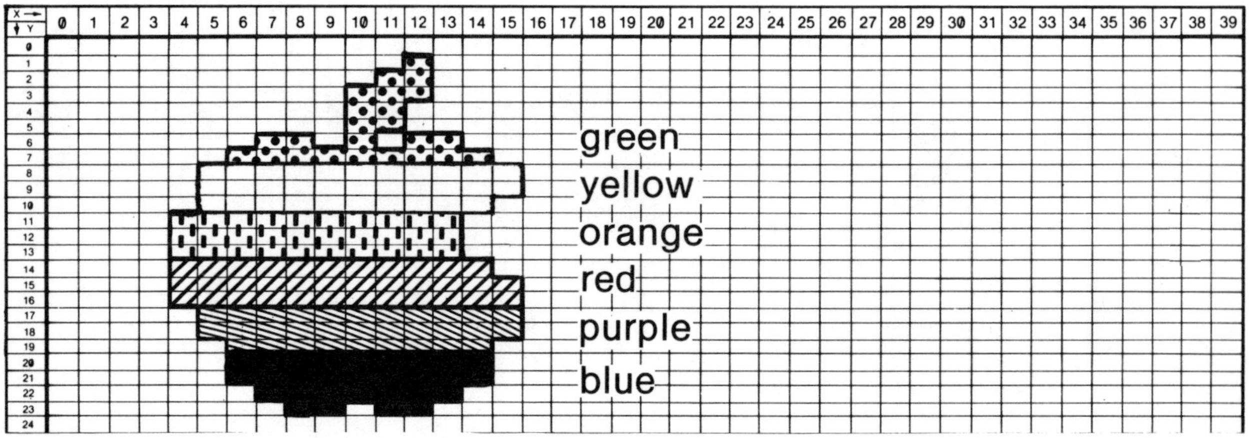

Drawing Vertical Lines

The Apple computer can draw vertical (up and down) lines on your display screen. The command VLIN is used for vertical lines.

This program draws an orange vertical line:

```
10 GR
20 COLOR = 9
30 VLIN 5, 11 AT 4
```

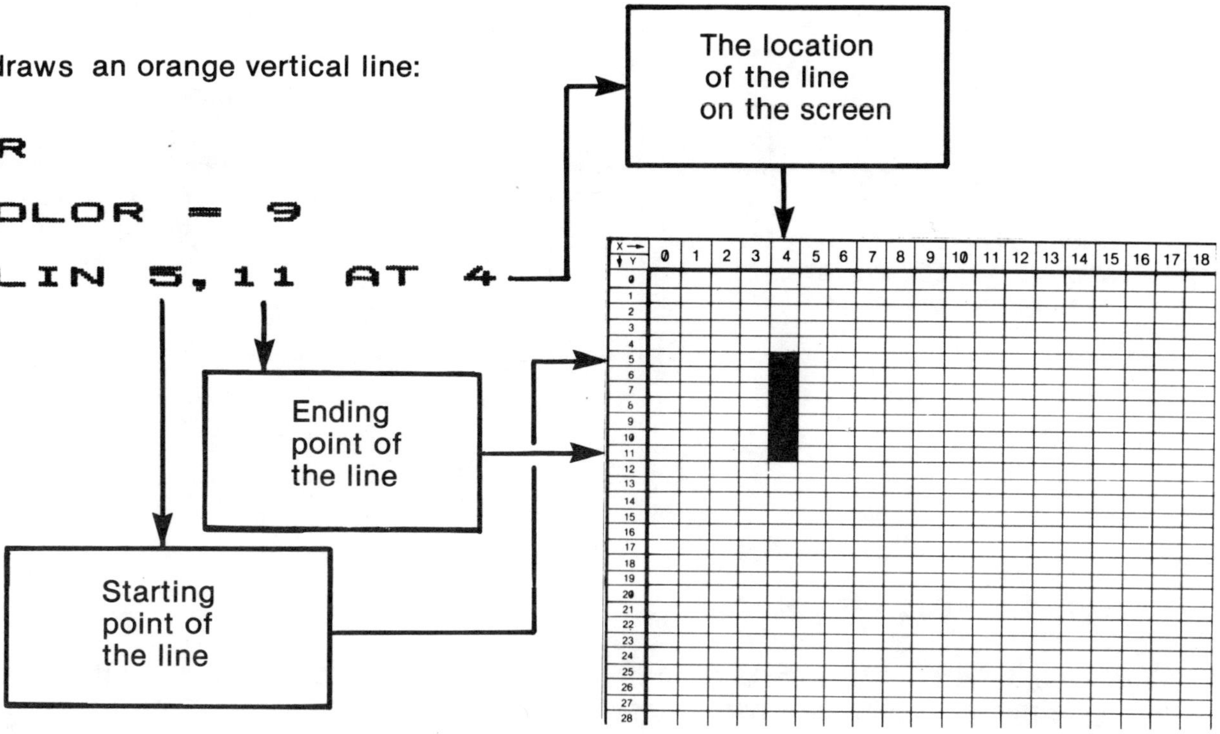

This program draws a yellow vertical line:

```
10 GR
20 COLOR = 13
30 VLIN 3, 12 AT 7
```

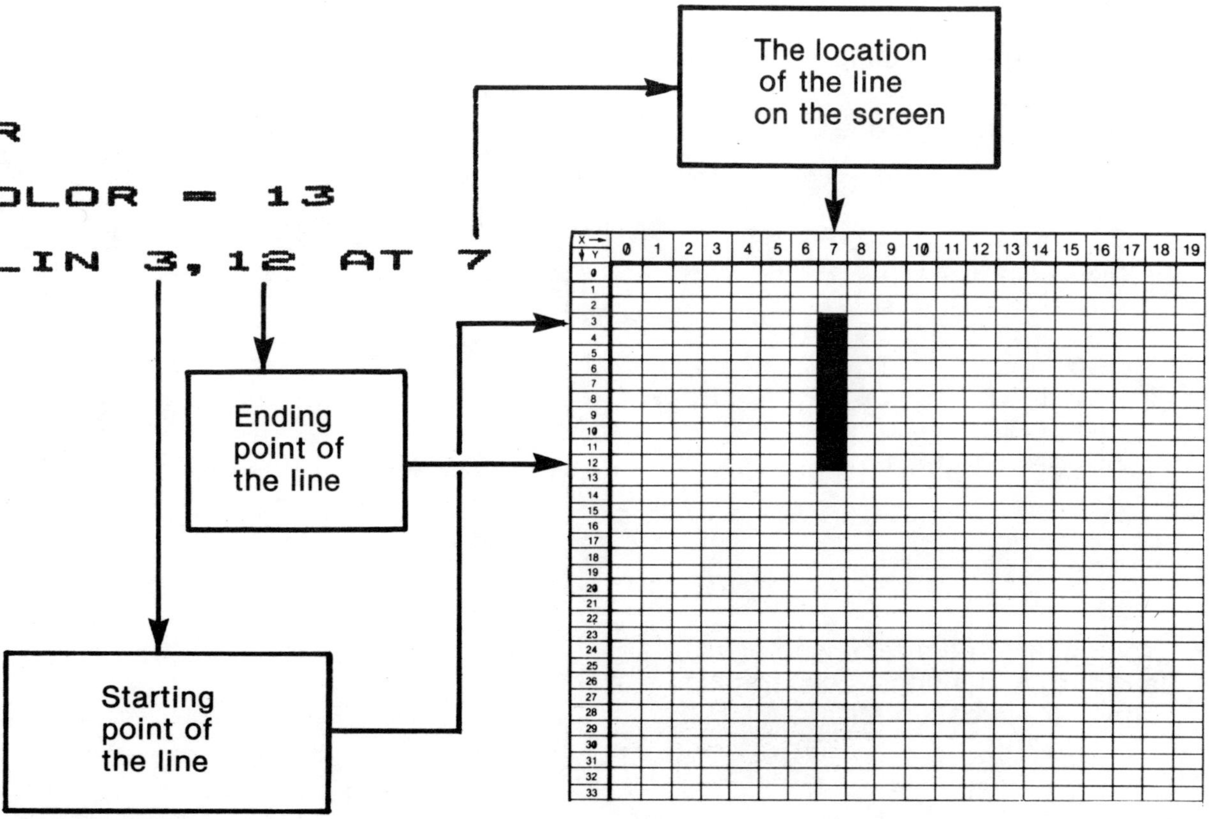

TRY THIS:

Look at the program and the picture. Each line number with a VLIN statement draws one of the vertical lines. Type in this program and RUN it.

```
100 GR
400 COLOR = 5
410 VLIN 12,16 AT 13
420 VLIN 12,16 AT 14
430 VLIN 12,21 AT 15
440 VLIN 12,21 AT 19
450 VLIN 12,16 AT 20
460 VLIN 12,16 AT 21
470 VLIN 17,21 AT 16
480 VLIN 17,22 AT 17
490 VLIN 17,21 AT 18
RUN
```

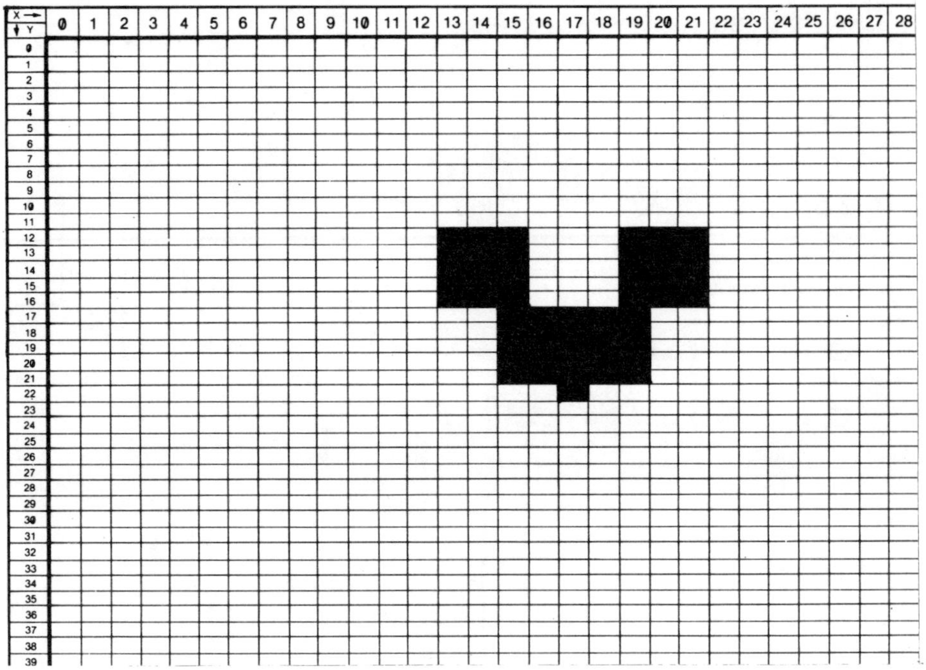

Drawing colors on colors

When you draw a cell of color over another color, the new color will show on the screen. The result is very similiar to cutting a paper design in one color and pasting it on a piece of paper of a different color.

TRY THIS:

Add the following lines to the program shown above:

```
510 COLOR = 11
520 VLIN 13,15 AT 20
530 VLIN 13,15 AT 14
540 COLOR = 8
550 PLOT 17,19
560 COLOR = 15
570 PLOT 16,18:PLOT 18,18
580 COLOR = 1
590 PLOT 17,21
RUN
```

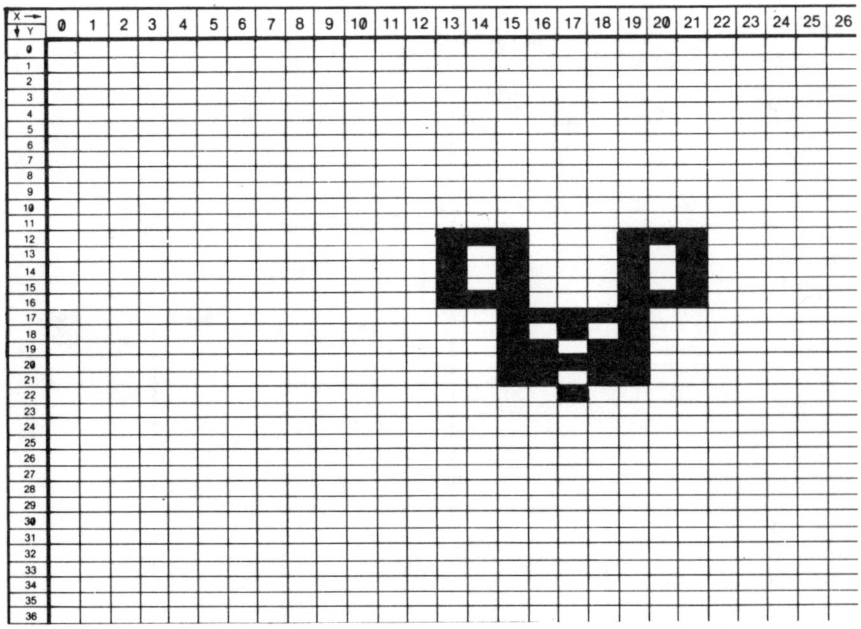

You should see a face with eyes, a mouth and a nose. This graphics character is called MICRO-MOUSE.

REMEMBER

YOU WILL BE USING THE PROGRAM LINES THAT DREW THE FACE OF MICRO-MOUSE LATER IN THIS LESSON. *YOU NEED TO SAVE THE PROGRAM TO DISK.* DIRECTIONS FOR SAVING PROGRAMS CAN BE FOUND INSIDE THE FRONT COVER. CALL THE PROGRAM *MICRO-MOUSE.*

Using REMARK (REM) statements

As you learn to write graphics programs, they will get longer and longer. Long programs need REM statements. REM stands for the work REMARK. REM statements are used to leave notes for the programmer.

One good reason to use REM statements in your program is that they are a reminder to you. After many HLIN, VLIN, and PLOT statements, it is easy to forget which part of the program drew which part of the figure. It is much easier to correct mistakes if your graphics program has REM statements in it. The program that drew the face of MICRO-MOUSE would look like this with REMS:

```
505 REM**DRAWS THE PINK IN THE EARS
510 COLOR = 11
520 VLIN 13,15 AT 20
530 VLIN 13,15 AT 14
535 REM**DRAWS THE NOSE
540 COLOR = 8
550 PLOT 17,19
555 REM**DRAWS EYES
560 COLOR = 15
570 PLOT 16,18:PLOT 18,18
575 REM**DRAWS MOUTH
580 COLOR = 1
590 PLOT 17,21
```

If one of your PLOT statements that draws the eyes was not correct, it would be easy to find. The REM statement in line 555 would tell you that the error is in line 570.

Computer Challenges

(1) Using HLIN, VLIN, COLOR = and PLOT statements, write a graphics program that will draw this sailboat. ONLY THE OUTLINE of the boat and the sail are shown. FILL in the outline to make the boat.

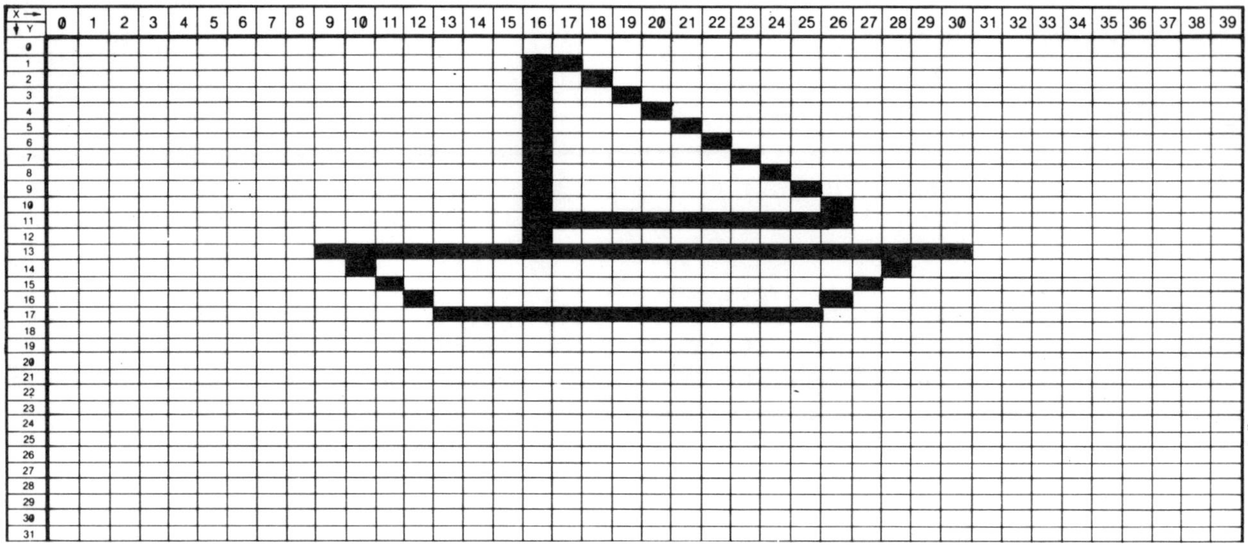

(2) Using HLIN, VLIN, COLOR = and PLOT statements, write a graphics program that will draw a body for MICRO-MOUSE.

Type LOAD MICRO-MOUSE and press <RETURN>. LIST the program.

Then add the lines to draw the body and the word MICRO-MOUSE. Use REM statements in your program.

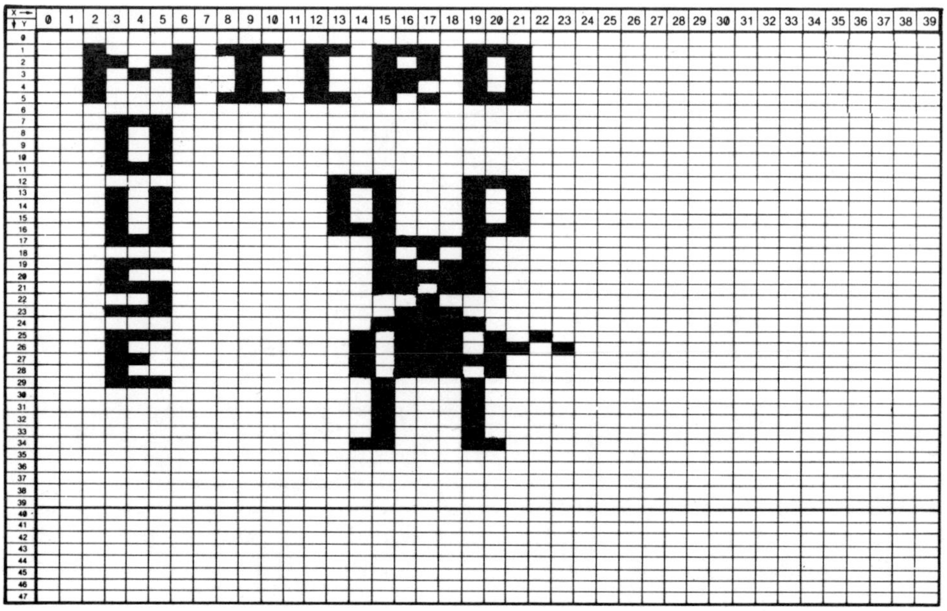

FOR-NEXT Loops and Graphics

This section is about the FOR-NEXT statement. It looks complicated but it is very easy to learn. Programmers use variables in FOR-NEXT loops. A variable is something that changes. A variable in our daily lives is the weather. It usually doesn't stay the same for long. In a computer program, we can assign a value to a variable. For example we could write

```
10 LET A = 10
```

We would be telling the computer to assign the value of 10 to the variable A. A variable can be any letter of the alphabet.

```
10 LET C = 20
20 LET W = 15
```

Have your parents ever said something like:

"FOR THE NEXT HOUR, I WANT SOME QUIET!"

Notice the words FOR and NEXT. The FOR-NEXT loop on a computer works like the statement your parents may have said.

TRY THIS:

Type in and RUN the two programs shown below:

```
10 GR
20 COLOR = 15
30 FOR X = 1 TO 6
40 HLIN 0,20 AT X
50 NEXT X
60 END
```

```
10 GR
20 COLOR = 15
30 HLIN 0,20 AT 1
40 HLIN 0,20 AT 2
50 HLIN 0,20 AT 3
60 HLIN 0,20 AT 4
70 HLIN 0,20 AT 5
80 HLIN 0,20 AT 6
90 END
```

Both programs do the same thing. The program on the left contains a FOR-NEXT LOOP. It has fewer line numbers than the one on the right. If you wanted the computer to draw 20 lines you could change lines 30 to (30 FOR X = 1 TO 20). You would have to add 14 more lines to the program on the right to do the same thing!

Look at the FOR-NEXT loop below:

```
10 GR
20 COLOR = 15
```

Beginning value for X. — Ending value for X.

```
30 FOR X = 1 TO 15
```

The number to start the loop. — The number of times to loop.

```
40 HLIN 0,10 AT X
50 NEXT X
```

What each line does

`10 GR`	(COMPUTER TO GRAPHICS MODE)
`20 COLOR = 15`	(USE WHITE AS A COLOR)
`30 FOR X = 1 TO 15`	(VARIABLE X WILL BE GIVEN THE VALUES OF 1 TO 15)
`40 HLIN 0,10 AT X`	(DRAW A LINE FROM 0 ACROSS THE SCREEN TO 10 AT THE LOCATION NAMED BY X)
`50 NEXT X`	(SEND THE COMPUTER TO THE BEGINNING OF THE LOOP IN LINE 30)

TRY THIS:

Change the ENDING VALUE for variable X in line 30. (30 FOR X = 1 TO 39) RUN the program again.

Change line 40 so the line is drawn completely across the screen (40 HLIN 0,39 AT X) and RUN the program.

Add this line number and command to your program:

```
45 GET A$
```

This statement causes the computer to wait until you press a key at the keyboard. It will let you see the HLIN's drawn one at a time. You will have to press a key such as the SPACE BAR over and over to see the lines drawn.

Drawing Squares and Rectangles

As you have discovered, you can change the size and location of a block of color by changing four values in the graphics program:

(1) The beginning value of the HLIN. (HLIN 0, 39 AT X)

(2) The ending value of the HLIN. (HLIN 0 , 39 AT X)

(3) The beginning value for the variable in the FOR part of the FOR-NEXT loop. (FOR X = 10 TO 19)

(4) The ending value for the variable in the FOR part of the FOR-NEXT loop. (FOR X = 10 TO 25)

TRY THIS:

Type in the following programs and RUN them.

```
10 GR                          (TURN ON GRAPHICS SCREEN)
20 COLOR = 15                  (COLOR TO USE IS WHITE)
30 FOR X = 0 TO 39             (START LOOP AT 0 & END AT 39)
40 HLIN 0,39 AT X              (DRAW HORIZONTAL LINE AT X)
50 NEXT X                      (LOOP BACK TO LINE 30)
```

The first FOR-NEXT loop draws horizontal lines that fill the screen. It is called a SCREEN WASH. (It fills the screen with one color).

```
60 COLOR = 1                   (COLOR TO USE IS RED)
70 FOR X = 5 TO 30             (START LOOP AT 5 & END AT 30)
80 HLIN 5,10 AT X              (DRAW HORIZONTAL LINE AT X)
90 NEXT X                      (LOOP BACK TO LINE 70)
100 END
```

Try changing the values in the FOR-NEXT loops to draw different sized blocks of color. The changes explained in *Drawing Squares and Rectangles* will help you.

Stepping into Stripes

If you want the computer to skip numbers instead of going to the next larger number in a loop, you can use the command STEP. Look at the next program:

```
10 GR
20 COLOR = 15
30 FOR X = 2 TO 38 STEP 2
40 HLIN 0,39 AT X
50 NEXT X
60 END
RUN
```

The FOR statement in line 30 has been changed. With the STEP command added to it, the program will count by twos (2,4,6,8,10,12,14 etc.) The computer begins at line 2 and draws a line. The NEXT X statement sends the computer back in a loop to line 30. The next value for X is 4 because STEP 2 has the computer count by twos.

TRY THIS:

Type in the program shown above and RUN it. Change the value of STEP in line 30 to other values such as 1 or 4. Try changing line 40 to a VLIN statement (i.e., 40 VLIN 0,39 AT X).

Fatter Stripes

The computer completes all the instructions between the FOR and the NEXT part of a loop. You can increase the thickness of the stripes by adding HLIN's between the FOR and the NEXT part of a loop.

TRY THIS:

Type in this program and RUN it:

```
10 GR                         (TURN ON GRAPHICS SCREEN)
20 COLOR = 15                 (COLOR TO USE IS WHITE)
30 FOR X = 10 TO 30 STEP 4    (START AT 10 AND COUNT BY
                               FOURS TO 30)
40 HLIN 0,39 AT X             (DRAW A HORIZONTAL LINE AT X)
50 HLIN 0,39 AT X + 1         (DRAW A SECOND LINE UNDER X)
60 HLIN 0,39 AT X + 2         (DRAW A THIRD LINE UNDER X)
70 NEXT X                     (LOOP BACK TO LINE 30)
80 END
```

Taking a Step Backwards

You can make the computer STEP backwards. The program is the same as the program on the bottom of page 22 except for line 30.

```
10 GR
20 COLOR = 15
30 FOR X = 30 TO 10 STEP -4
40 HLIN 0,39 AT X
50 HLIN 0,39 AT X + 1
60 HLIN 0,39 AT X + 2
80 NEXT X
90 END
```

Line 30 has the computer count from 30 to 10. The STEP -4 has it count by fours, (30,26,22,18 etc.) The STEP -4 has the computer subtract four each time the loop is completed.

Delay Loops

The screen fills with stripes very quickly. It is difficult to tell if the computer fills the screen from bottom to top or from the top down.

TRY THIS:

Add this line to your program:

```
70 FOR D = 1 TO 200:NEXT D
```

Your program should look like this:

```
10 GR
20 COLOR = 15
30 FOR X = 30 TO 10 STEP -4
40 HLIN 0,39 AT X
50 HLIN 0,39 AT X + 1
60 HLIN 0,39 AT X + 2
70 FOR D = 1 TO 200:NEXT D
80 NEXT X
90 END
```

Line 70 is called a DELAY LOOP. Line 70 has the computer stop and COUNT TO 200 BEFORE GOING TO THE NEXT LINE. It is a FOR-NEXT loop that only counts. The time that it takes the computer to count is the DELAY. Try changing the ending value for variable D in line 70. Make it larger (70 D = 1 to 1000:NEXT D) or make it smaller (70 D = 1 to 50:NEXT D).

(1) Write a program that uses a FOR-NEXT loop to fill the mug with water. The first part of the program is completed for you.

(Hint—You will want to fill the mug from the bottom up. The FOR-NEXT loop will have a beginning value of 30 and an ending value of 12. It will need a STEP -1.)

```
10 REM**PROGRAM TO FILL MUG WITH WATER
20 GR
30 COLOR = 15
40 REM**DRAWS MUG
50 VLIN 10,31 AT 9
60 VLIN 10,31 AT 17
70 HLIN 9,17 AT 31
80 VLIN 16,24 AT 21
90 HLIN 18,19 AT 14
100 HLIN 18,19 AT 26
110 PLOT 20,15
120 PLOT 20,25
130 REM**FOR-NEXT LOOP TO FILL MUG
```

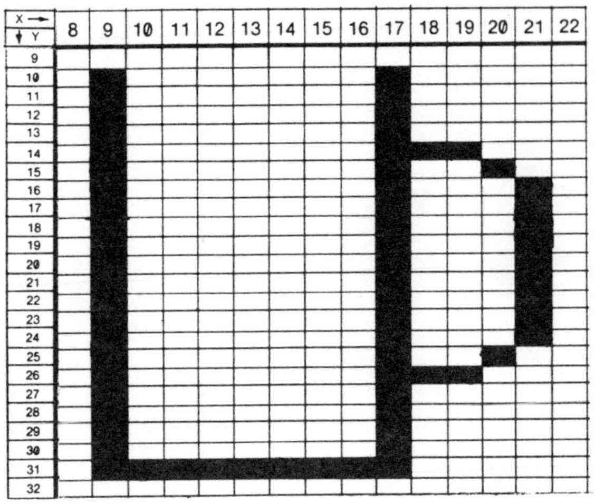

(2) Write a program that uses a FOR-NEXT loop to color the screen white from line 0 to line 39.

Use a second FOR-NEXT loop to draw blue stripes (three HLIN's thick) from line 0 to line 35. You will need a STEP by 5. (See Fatter Stripes on Page 22.)

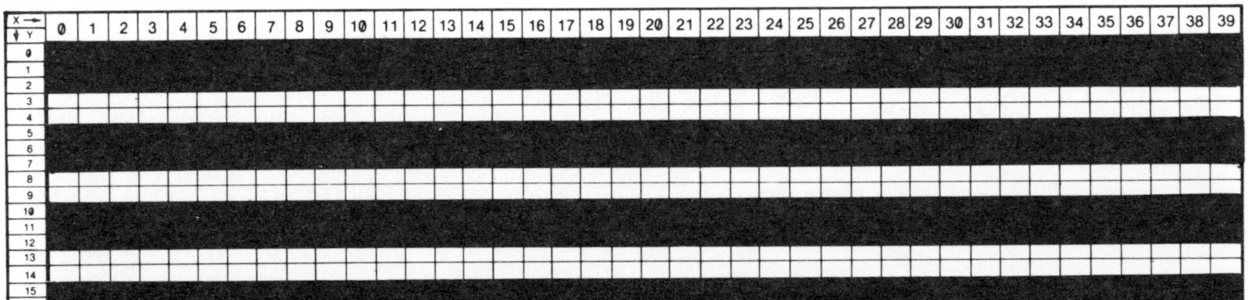

APPLE GRAPHICS

STATEMENTS

GR–sets the stage for low-res graphics

COLOR–sets the color

PLOT–place a block at a specified location

HLIN–used to draw horizontal lines

VLIN–used to draw vertical lines

TEXT–clears the graphics mode

APPLESOFT COLORS

Ø	black
1	magenta
2	dark blue
3	purple
4	dark green
5	gray
6	medium blue
7	light blue
8	brown
9	orange
1Ø	gray
11	pink
12	green
13	yellow
14	aqua
15	white

Draw a red rectangle of color at the center of the flag. Look closely at the numbers on the grid to see where it should start and end.

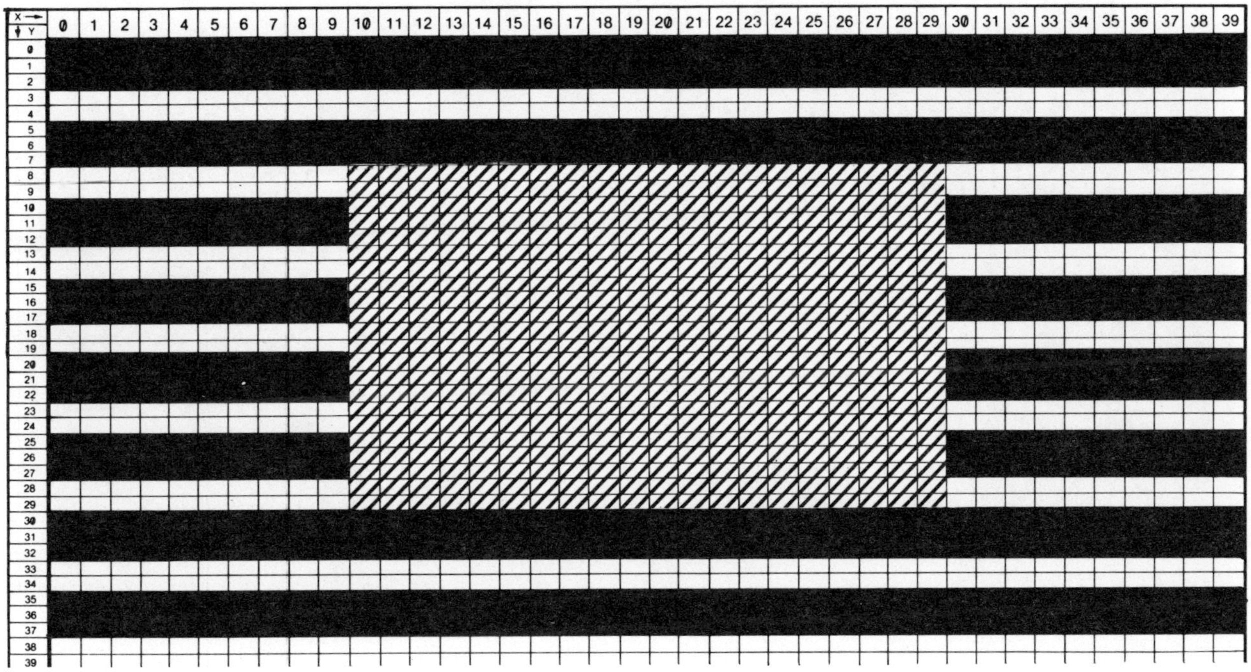

Using a FOR-NEXT loop draw six white horizontal lines in the rectangle. (Hint: The FOR-NEXT loop should start at 11 and end at 26 and STEP by 3)

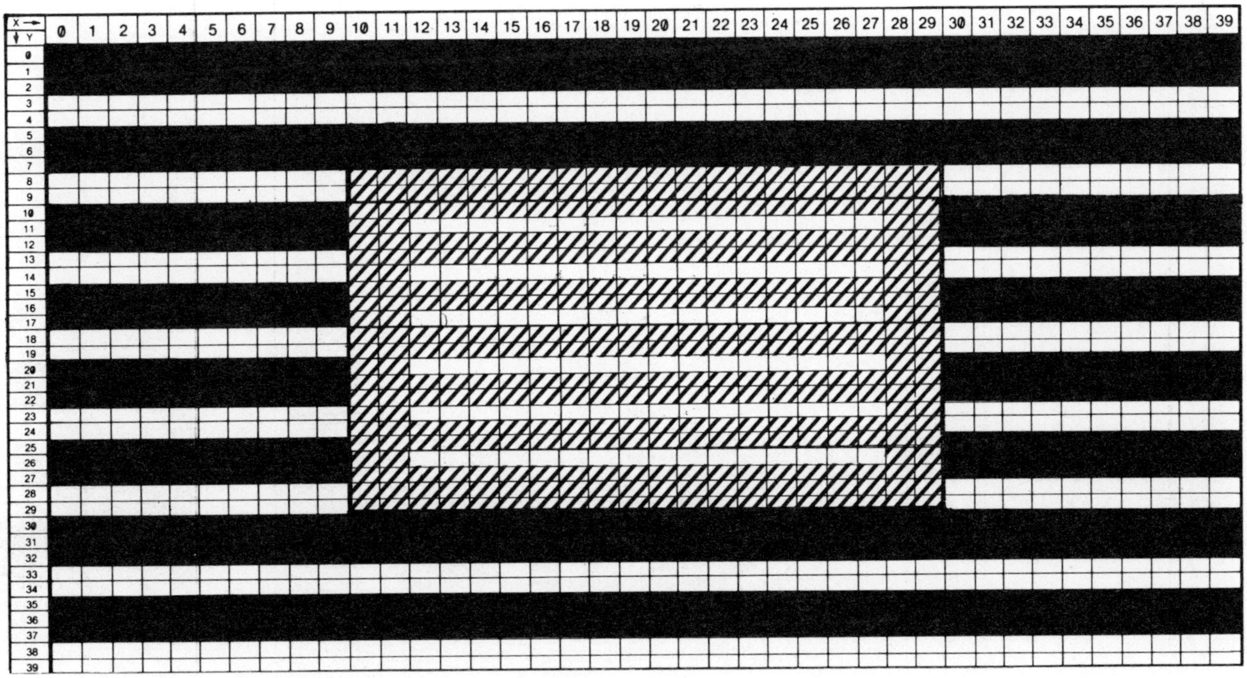

Using a FOR-NEXT loop draw six VLIN's across the red rectangle.

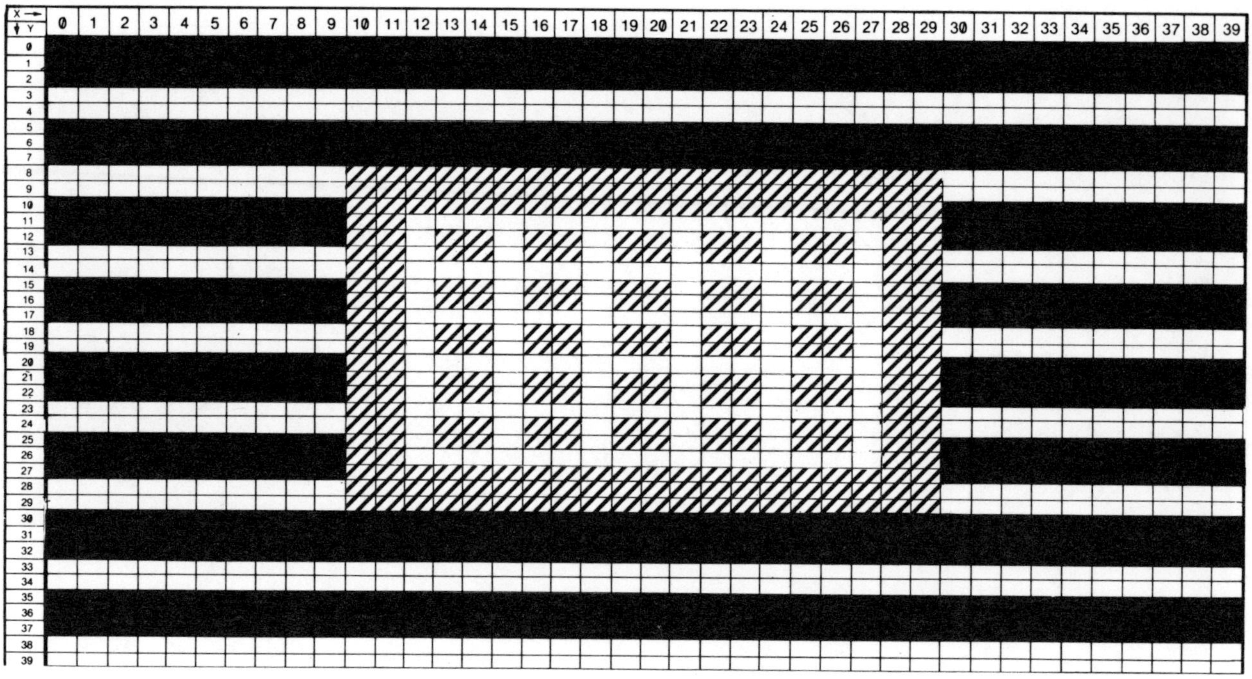

Use two HLIN's and two VLIN's to draw a blue cross in the center of the red rectangle. The graphics picture is a flag. You may want to draw a flag of your choice as your next project.

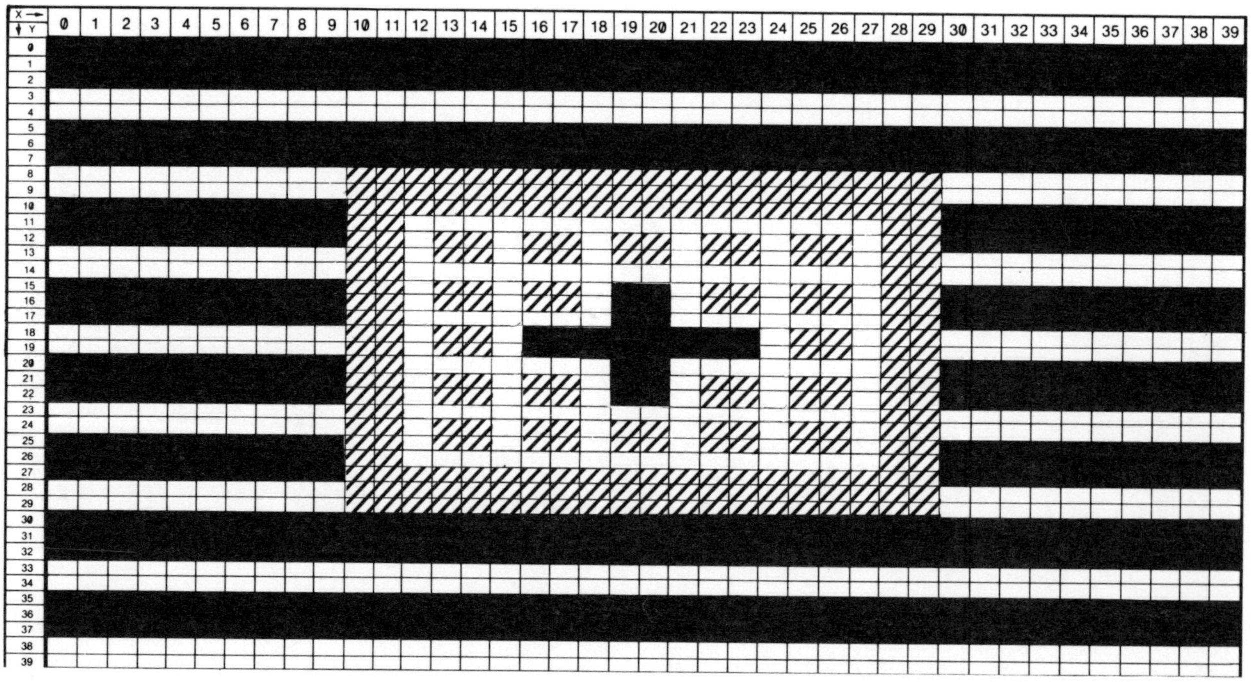

Diagonal Plots

The graphics screen has two directions that are important in drawing a cell of color on the screen.

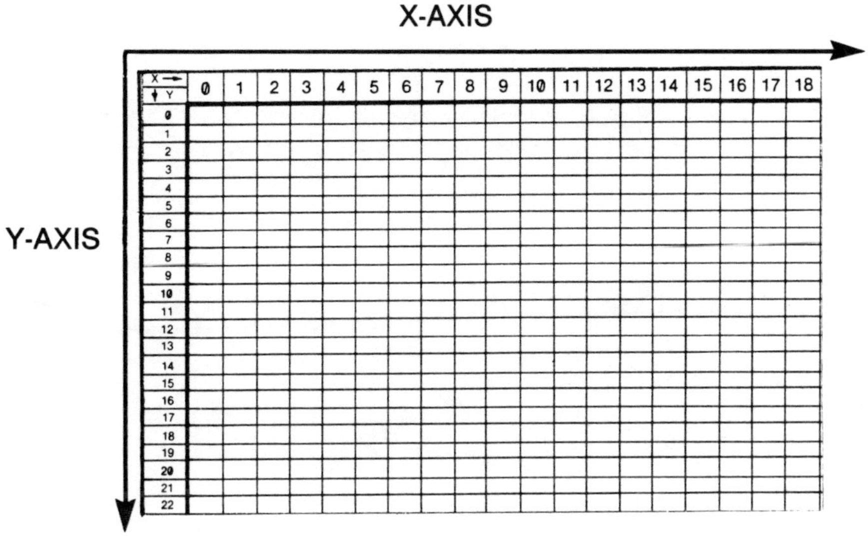

One is across the screen (side to side). The other is the up and down direction. The side-to-side direction is called the X-AXIS. The up and down direction is called the Y-AXIS.

To get the computer to draw a diagonal line, you must follow these steps:

(1) Use a FOR-NEXT loop to draw cells of color across the screen from left to right (X-AXIS)

(2) Increase the value of Y inside the FOR-NEXT loop. This moves the PLOT location down the Y-AXIS.

TRY THIS:

Type in the following program and RUN it.

`10 GR`	(TURN ON GRAPHICS SCREEN)
`20 Y = 0`	(SET THE FIRST VERTICAL-UP AND DOWN-VALUE AT 0. TOP OF SCREEN.)
`30 COLOR = 15`	(COLOR TO USE IS WHITE)
`40 FOR X = 0 TO 39`	(START LOOP AT LEFT SIDE OF SCREEN AND MOVE RIGHT 39 TIMES)
`50 PLOT X,Y`	(PLOT A CELL OF COLOR AT EACH NEW X AND Y POSITION)
`60 Y = Y + 1`	(MAKE THE VALUE OF Y INCREASE BY ONE. THIS MOVES THE PLOT LOCATION DOWN THE SCREEN)
`70 NEXT X`	(LOOP BACK TO LINE 40)
`80 END`	

Computer Challenges

(1) Using the program on page 27 as a model, write a program that draws a diagonal line from 10,10 to 20,20. You will need to change the values in lines 20 and 40.

(2) Using two FOR-NEXT loops, draw an 'X' across the screen.

(Hint—You will have to reset the value of Y to 0 (Y = 0) before you begin the second loop. You will have to use STEP -1 in the loop that PLOTS the line from upper right to lower left.)

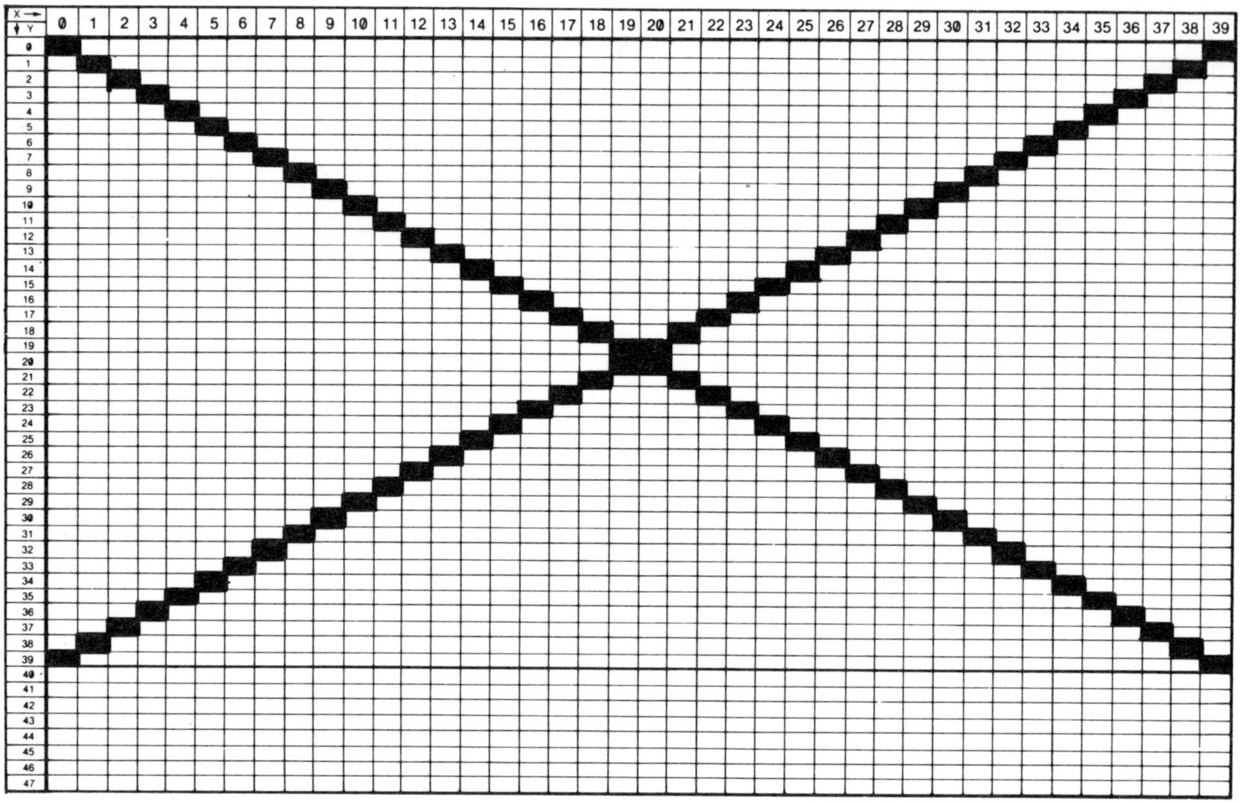

Flash

Showing movement with graphics figures is called animation. Writing a program that includes movement is not difficult. Simple graphics programs with animation are based on this simple principle:

DRAW — ERASE — DRAW

TRY THIS:

Type in this program and RUN it. The program will work just as well without the REM statements.

```
10 REM**CLOWN FACE**
20 GR
30 REM**DRAWS SMILE**
40 COLOR = 1
50 PLOT 16,28:PLOT 17,29
60 HLIN 18,20 AT 30
70 PLOT 21,29:PLOT 22,28
80 REM**DRAWS NOSE**
90 COLOR = 11
100 HLIN 18,20 AT 26:HLIN 18,20 AT 27
110 REM**DRAWS EYEBROWS**
120 COLOR = 15
130 PLOT 16,22:PLOT 17,21
140 PLOT 18,22:PLOT 20,22
150 PLOT 21,21:PLOT 22,22
160 REM**DRAWS EYES**
170 COLOR = 7
180 PLOT 17,24:PLOT 21,24
190 REM**DELAY LOOP TO SHOW PICTURE
    WITH EYES**
200 FOR D = 1 TO 1000:NEXT D
210 REM**ERASE EYE BY DRAWING IT AS
    BACKGROUND COLOR
220 COLOR = 0
230 PLOT 17,24
240 REM**DELAY TO SHOW EYE WINKING**
250 FOR D = 1 TO 1000:NEXT D
260 GOTO 170
```

You have to press the <CTRL> key (hold it down) and press the <C> key to stop the program.

The GOTO in line 260 keeps sending the computer back to line 170 until you stop the program with <CTRL> <C>.

You could select COLOR = 0 and plot the edges of the smile. If you drew them again with COLOR = 15 as a frown, the clown would seem to smile and then frown.

In some programs, a programmer would like to have the Apple computer select random colors. Random means that something happens by chance. For example, when you choose members for a team from numbers placed in a hat, you are selecting them in a random way.

Apple has a RND function. RND stands for random. The Apple computer can choose numbers at random but it needs to know the number range. For example, there are 15 colors (not including black) that it can choose from. The range is 1 to 15. A graphics statement for selecting a random number from 1 through 15 looks like this:

Variable — Ending number — Beginning number

```
10 C = INT(15*RND(1)) + 1
```

TRY THIS:

```
10 C = INT(15*RND(1)) + 1
20 PRINT "THE NUMBER IS  "; C
30 GOTO 10
```

The program assigns a value from 1 through 15 to variable C. Line 20 prints this value. Line 30 tells the computer to go back to line 10.The command GOTO is used when you want the computer to GOTO some line number other than the next larger one in a program.

You must press <CTRL> and <C> keys to stop this program.

TRY THIS:

Type in this program and RUN it.

```
10 GR
20 C = INT(15*RND(1)) + 1
30 COLOR = C
40 X = INT(15*RND(1)) + 1
50 Y = INT(15*RND(1)) + 1
60 PLOT X,Y
70 GOTO 20
```

Let the program continue for a few minutes. The colors and the locations to PLOT the colors are being randomly chosen.

Press <CTRL> and <C> key to stop the program.

TRY THIS:

Type in and RUN this program:

```
10 REM**CHRISTMAS TREE**
20 GR
30 COLOR = 4
40 PLOT 20,0
50 HLIN 19,21 AT 1
60 HLIN 19,21 AT 2
70 HLIN 18,22 AT 3
80 HLIN 18,22 AT 4
90 HLIN 17,23 AT 5
100 HLIN 16,24 AT 6
110 FOR X = 1 TO 100
120 REM**RANDOM COLORS**
130 C = INT(15*RND(1)) + 1
140 COLOR = C
150 PLOT 20,0:PLOT 22,2
160 C = C + 1
170 PLOT 20,3:PLOT 22,6
180 C = C + 2
190 PLOT 17,4:PLOT 18,2
200 PLOT 19,6
210 REM**DELAY LOOP**
220 FOR D = 1 TO 1000:NEXT D
230 NEXT X
```

This program draws a small Christmas tree with lights. The color of the lights is randomly chosen. The value of the color is assigned to variable C. Line 140 sets the COLOR = C. The random number for color is PLOTTED. In lines 160 and 180 the computer adds one or two to the color value. This gives the next PLOT statement a new color.

(1) Using HLIN and PLOT commands write a program that draws a JACK-O-LANTERN. Add the lines that will make its eyes flash from black to yellow.

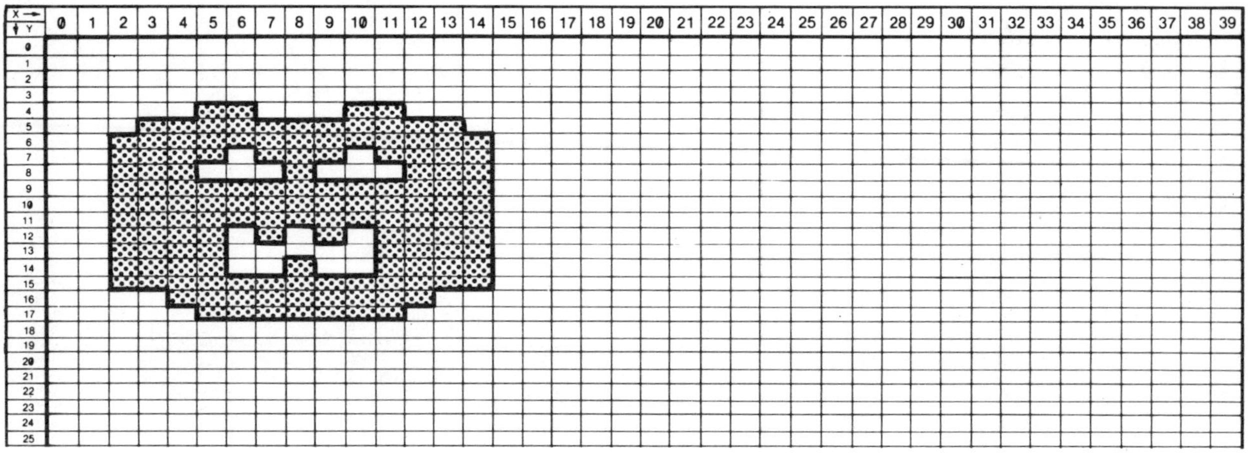

(2) Using HLIN and FOR-NEXT loops write a program that draws a traffic control signal. The blocks of colors for the lights flash from GREEN to YELLOW to RED. The block of color should change to gray after it flashes.

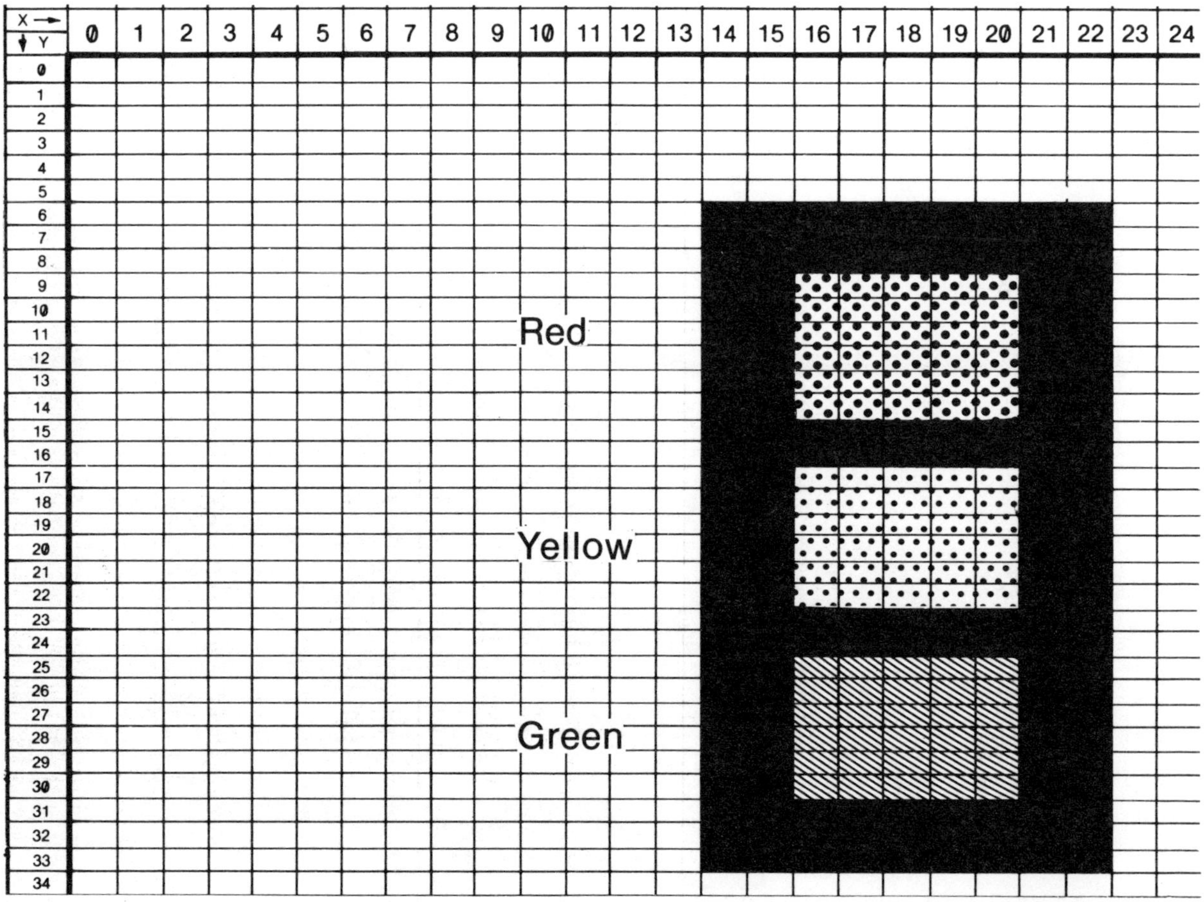

Graphics Animation

The secret to drawing objects that move is simple. You draw them the same color as the background color and redraw them in a new location.

This program moves a block of color across the screen.

```
10 GR
20 FOR X = 0 TO 39
30 COLOR = 15:REM**DRAW**
40 PLOT X,Y
50 FOR P = 1 TO 50:NEXT P
60 COLOR = 0:REM**ERASE**
70 PLOT X,Y
80 NEXT X
```

TRY THIS:

Type in the program above and RUN it.

Add these lines:

```
90 FOR X = 39 TO 0 STEP -1
100 COLOR = 15:REM**DRAW**
110 PLOT X,Y
120 FOR P = 1 TO 50:NEXT P
130 COLOR = 0:REM*ERASE**
140 PLOT X,Y
150 NEXT X
160 GOTO 20
```

The graphics program is telling the computer to:

LINE 20	Go from the left side of the screen (0) to the right (39)
LINE 40	Plot a cell of color at X,Y (Y = 0)
LINE 50	Pause to keep the cell drawn on the screen
LINE 60-70	Erase the cell by drawing it as background color
LINE 80	Return to line 20 until the cell of color has been drawn 40 times
LINE 90	Go from the right side of the screen (39) to the left (0)
LINE 100 TO LINE 150	Do the same things as lines 30 to 70 but in the opposite direction (STEP -1)
LINE 160	Sends the computer back to LINE 20 to do it all again.

GOSUB-RETURN

Two new statements in BASIC can help you animate your pictures. GOSUB and RETURN are like FOR-NEXT. If you use the GOSUB command, you must have a RETURN. GOSUB-RETURN is used in a program when you want the computer to jump to another place in the program to perform some task and return to its original place.

In graphics animation we draw—erase—draw in a new location. To get the cell of color to move on page 33, we typed very similar instructions twice. LINES 30 to 70 and LINES 100 to 140 are the same. If we had used GOSUB-RETURN we could have saved typing in the duplicate program lines.

```
10 GR
20 FOR X = 0 TO 39
30 GOSUB 90
40 NEXT X
50 FOR X = 39 TO 0 STEP -1
60 GOSUB 90
70 NEXT X
80 END
90 COLOR = 15
100 PLOT X,Y
110 FOR P = 1 TO 50:NEXT P
120 COLOR = 0
130 PLOT X,Y
140 RETURN
```

SUBROUTINE

TRY THIS:

Type in the program above and RUN it.

Change line 80 to 80 GOTO 20

Try changing lines 100 and 130 to draw a vertical line.
For example, make both lines VLIN 10,20 AT X

Try changing only line 130 to VLIN 14,18 AT X

****

REMEMBER

It is important to remember these rules about GOSUB-RETURN:

(1) The GOSUB statement causes the computer to branch to a subroutine.

(2) The RETURN sends the computer back to the instructions immediately following the original GOSUB statement.

****

The listing below shows two subroutines. They are located at lines 300 and 400.

`5 HOME`	
`10 REM**JUMPING JACK**`	
`20 GR`	
`30 COLOR = 15`	
`40 VLIN 17,19 AT 18`	
`50 VLIN 17,24 AT 19`	
`60 VLIN 17,19 AT 20`	Draws parts of the figure that do not move.
`70 HLIN 17,21 AT 21`	
`80 HLIN 18,20 AT 22`	
`90 HLIN 18,20 AT 23`	
`100 HLIN 18,20 AT 24`	
`110 HLIN 10,30 AT 29`	Draws the ground.
`120 GOSUB 300`	Goes to line 300 to draw figure standing.
`130 FOR P = 1 TO 200:NEXT P`	A longer pause.
`140 COLOR = 0:REM**MAKES COLOR = BACKGROUND COLOR**`	
`150 GOSUB 300`	Goes to line 300 to erase standing legs.
`160 COLOR = 15:REM**MAKES COLOR = WHITE**`	
`170 GOSUB 400`	Goes to line 400 to draw legs apart.
`180 FOR P = 1 TO 50:NEXT P`	A short pause.
`190 COLOR = 0`	
`200 GOSUB 400`	Erase legs apart.
`210 GOTO 30`	Go to line 30.
`300 VLIN 25,28 AT 18`	
`310 VLIN 25,28 AT 20`	SUBROUTINE to draw figure standing.
`320 PLOT 16,22:PLOT 15,23`	
`330 PLOT 22,22:PLOT 23,23`	
`340 PLOT 21,28:PLOT 17,28`	
`350 RETURN`	
`400 PLOT 18,25:PLOT 20,25`	
`410 PLOT 21,26:PLOT 22,27`	SUBROUTINE to draw legs apart and arms up.
`420 PLOT 17,26:PLOT 16,27`	
`430 VLIN 18,20 AT 16`	
`440 VLIN 18,20 AT 22`	
`450 RETURN`	

TRY THIS:

Type in the program and RUN it.

Computer Challenges

(1) Using HLIN, VLIN, and GOSUB-RETURN statements, draw a picture of a blue flashlight that switches on a yellow light and then switches off. Look at the example below.

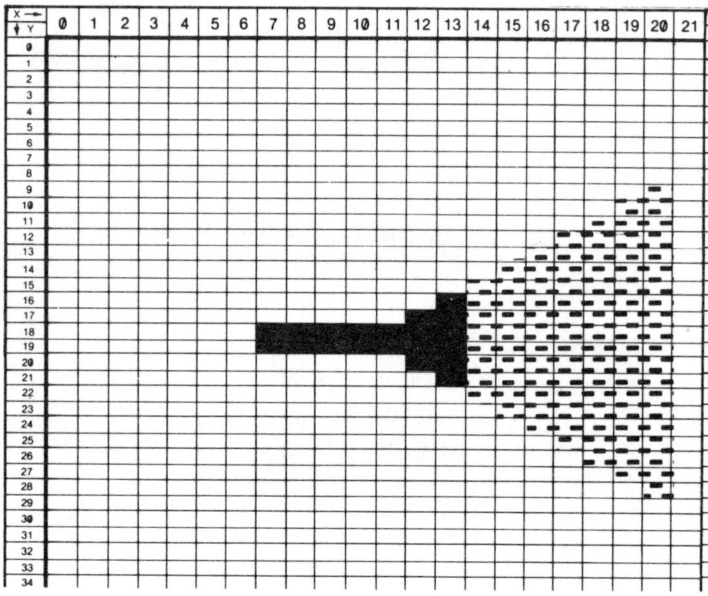

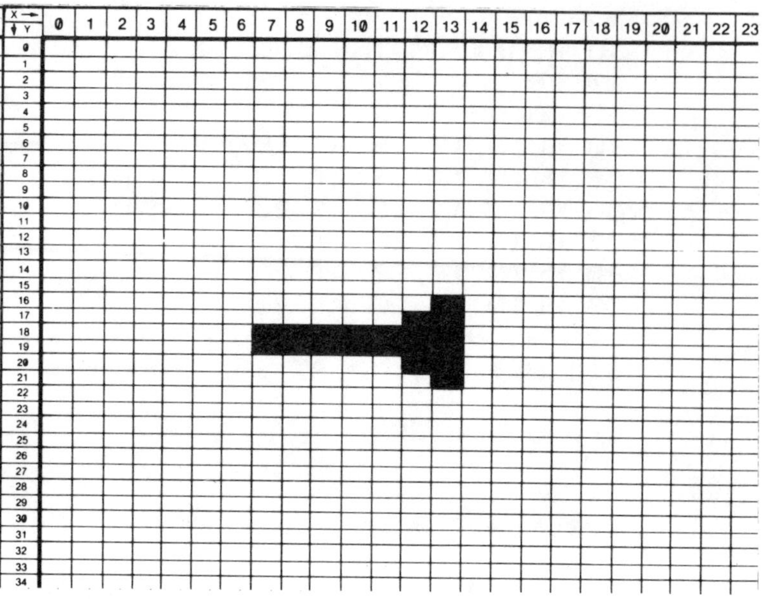

(2) Using FOR-NEXT loops, VLIN, HLIN, GOSUB-RETURN, and RND statements, draw a VOLCANO. The volcano should erupt with a cloud of ash above the mountain.

HINTS:

(1) The eruption should occur in stages with the ash cloud getting larger.

(2) The routines that draw the ash in various stages should be in subroutines.

(3) You may want to change the colors of the eruption.

(4) Delay loops should separate the parts of the eruption.

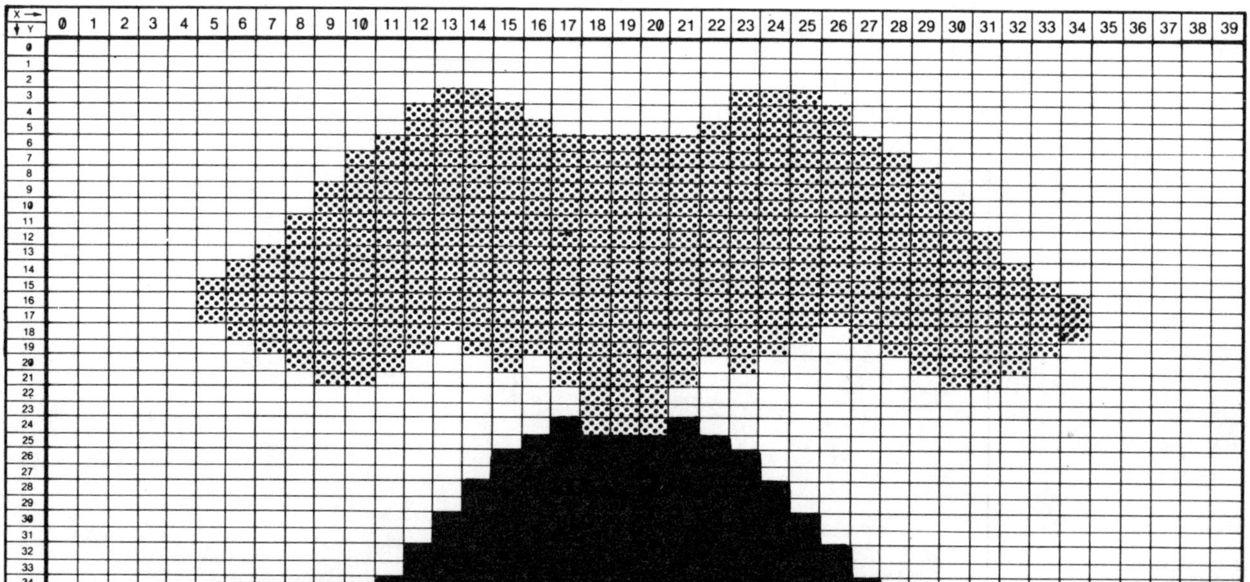

READ / DATA in Graphics

You have already seen that variables in a program can be assigned values by using LET or FOR-NEXT.

```
LET A = 4                                  FOR X = 1 TO 15
```

Another way to assign values to variables uses two statements: READ and DATA.

Program:

```
10 READ X
20 PRINT "X IS NOW ";X
30 GOTO 10
40 DATA 12,122,36,8
RUN
```

Output:

```
X IS NOW 12
X IS NOW 122
X IS NOW 36
X IS NOW 8
OUT OF DATA ERROR
```

Line 10 tells the computer to READ one value from the DATA line. The first value (12) is assigned to X.

Line 20 prints 12 (the value of X).

Line 30 sends the computer back to line 10 to READ the next value of X.

This program gives an error message: OUT OF DATA ERROR. To avoid this, the program must contain a "flag" to tell the computer when to stop trying to READ more DATA.

```
10 READ X
20 IF X = 999 THEN END <- - - - - - - - - - - FLAG
30 PRINT "X NOW HAS THIS VALUE ";X
40 GOTO 10
50 DATA 12,22,36,8,999
```

Line 20 tells the computer to make a decision. IF the value assigned to X is 999 THEN END the program. When X = 999 the program ends.

TRY THIS:

Type in the program shown above and RUN it.

Change the numbers in the DATA line and RUN the program again.

READ / DATA Statements and PLOT

READ/DATA statements can be used in graphics programs. They can make graphics programs easier to type. Instead of many PLOT statements, you can type in DATA lines.

```
10 GR
20 COLOR = 15
30 READ A,B ←————————————————— LINE 30 READS 2 DATA
                                VALUES AT A TIME

40 IF A = 999 OR B = 999 THEN END
50 PLOT A,B
60 GOTO 30
70 DATA 6,17,5,18,4,19
80 DATA 5,20,6,21,7,20
90 DATA 8,19,7,18,999,999
```

TRY THIS:

Type in and RUN the program shown above.
Change the DATA values in the DATA line to draw a triangle.

READ / DATA Statements with HLIN & VLIN

HLIN and VLIN statements need three values to be drawn on the screen:

(1) A beginning value to be drawn from.
(2) An ending value to be drawn to.
(3) An AT location on the screen.

```
HLIN        10, 20 AT 8
VLIN        9 , 15 AT 5
```

READ/DATA statements can be used to draw lines on the video screen. The READ statement will read the three shown above.

```
10 GR
20 COLOR = 9
30 READ A,B,C
40 IF A = 999 OR B = 999
   OR C = 999 THEN END
50 HLIN A,B AT C
60 GOTO 30
70 DATA 7,8,24,5,10,25
80 DATA 4,11,26,5,10,27
90 DATA 7,8,28,999,999,999
```

TRY THIS:

Type in the program and RUN it. Change the DATA values in the DATA statement.
Change LINE 50 to 50 VLIN A,B AT C and RUN the program.

READ/DATA statements can use HLIN and VLIN statements with random colors to draw patterns:

```
10 GR
20 C = INT(15*RND(1)) + 1
30 COLOR = C
40 READ A,B,C
50 IF A = 999 OR B = 999 OR
   C = 999 THEN END
60 HLIN A,B AT C
70 VLIN B,A AT C
80 GOTO 20
90 DATA 10,20,10,8,18,8,6,16,6
100 DATA 4,14,4,999,999,999
```

TRY THIS:

Type in the program above and RUN it. Change the DATA values in LINES 90 and 100.

READ/DATA statements can be used to READ alphabet characters (A,B,C,D, etc) as well as numbers.

```
5 HOME
10 GR
20 COLOR = 7
30 X = 10:Y = 10
40 READ A$,X,Y
50 IF A$ = "END" THEN END
60 PLOT X,Y
70 PRINT A$;
80 FOR P = 1 TO 700:NEXT P
90 GOTO 40
100 DATA THIS ,10,10, IS ,10,11
110 DATA THE ,10,12, LETTER ,10,13
120 DATA L,11,13  END,0,0
```

(Line 40 ←) THE FIRST VALUE READ IS AN ALPHABET CHARACTER.

Pay special attention to line 40. The computer READs 3 values from the DATA lines at a time. When the computer READs words or letters of the alphabet from the DATA line, the variable (A$ in line 40) must have a $. The $ tells the computer to expect alphabet characters instead of numbers. You must be careful how you put spaces in the DATA lines or your words may run together.

TRY THIS:

Type in and RUN the program shown above.
Change the DATA lines so the computer draws the letter 'A'.

Putting it all Together

This program uses READ/DATA, a flag, and GOSUB-RETURN FOR-NEXT loops, and IF-THEN statements to create graphic movement:

```
5 HOME
10 GR
20 X = 20:Y = 20                  <----  FIRST LOCATION FOR X AND Y
30 READ X$,N,Y$                   <----  READ THREE DATA STATEMENTS
40 IF Y$ = "Z" THEN END           <----  FLAG TO END OF PROGRAM
50 FOR Z = 1 TO N                 <----  BEGINNING OF FOR-NEXT LOOP
60 GOSUB 140                      <----  GO TO SUBROUTINE AT LINE 140
70 COLOR = 15                     <----  COLOR TO USE IS WHITE
80 PLOT X,Y                       <----  PLOT CELL ON SCREEN
90 FOR P = 1 TO 75:NEXT P         <----  DELAY LOOP
100 COLOR = 0                     <----  MAKE COLOR = BACKGROUND
110 PLOT X,Y                      <----  ERASE CELL ON SCREEN
120 NEXT Z                        <----  GO BACK TO LINE 50 N TIMES
130 GOTO 30
140 IF X$ = "L" THEN X = X - 1    <----  SUBROUTINE TO CHANGE THE
150 IF X$ = "R" THEN X = X + 1           VALUE OF X AND Y TO MOVE
160 IF Y$ = "U" THEN Y = Y - 1           THE CELL OF COLOR LEFT,
170 IF Y$ = "D" THEN Y = Y + 1           RIGHT, UP OR DOWN
180 IF X$ = "S" THEN X = X
190 IF Y$ = "S" THEN Y = Y
200 RETURN                        <----  GO BACK TO LINE 70
210 DATA L,10,S                   <----  DATA STATEMENTS
220 DATA R,10,S                          L MEANS MOVE LEFT
230 DATA S,5,D                           NUMBER TELLS HOW MANY TIMES
240 DATA L,6,S                           TO MOVE UP, DOWN, RIGHT OR LEFT
250 DATA S,10,U                          R MEANS MOVE RIGHT
260 DATA R,10,U                          U MEANS MOVE UP
270 DATA 0,0,Z                           D MEANS MOVE DOWN
                                         S MEANS SAME LOCATION
```

TRY THIS:

Type in the program and RUN it.

You can change the data statements to move the cell of color. For example, 240 DATA L, 6 ,S tells the computer to move left 6 spaces at the same vertical location.

The DATA statements can be LONGER than the ones shown in the program. You could combine lines 210,220 and 230 into one DATA statement:

210 DATA L,10,S,R,10,S,S,5,D

Correcting Errors

If you get a ?ILLEGAL QUANTITY ERROR message, you will probably have to change one of your DATA statements.

?ILLEGAL QUANTITY ERROR IN 80 or 110 does not mean that the problem is in these line numbers. The DATA statements are incorrect. The computer is trying to draw a cell of color off the screen. The graphics screen is 40 cells wide and 40 cells up and down. You cannot exceed 39 because the computer starts counting at 0. When the computer has counted to 39, it has counted 40 times. An easy way to see this is to count the fingers on one hand. The first finger is 0 and the last finger will be counted as 4.

You can find an error in the DATA statements by adding this line

```
95 PRINT X$,N,Y$
```

When the error happens, the values from the DATA statements will be shown on the screen.

TRY THIS:

Change line 110 to `PLOT X,Y:PLOT X+1,Y`

Change the length of the delay loop in line 90

Try deleting line 90

Try changing the values of X and Y in LINE 20

Try changing the values of X and Y in LINES 140 and 150.

```
140 IF X$ = "L" THEN X = X - 2
150 IF X$ = "R" THEN X = X + 2
```

Try changing the DATA statements to move the dot of color in different paths around the screen.

Computer Challenges

(1) Use the READ/DATA program on page 38 as a model. Write a graphics program with READ/DATA that will draw your initials on the screen.

(2) Using HLIN and VLIN statements draw the AQUARIUM. Using FOR-NEXT loop, fill the aquarium with blue water. Using the program on page 40, draw a gold fish that swims in different paths in the aquarium.

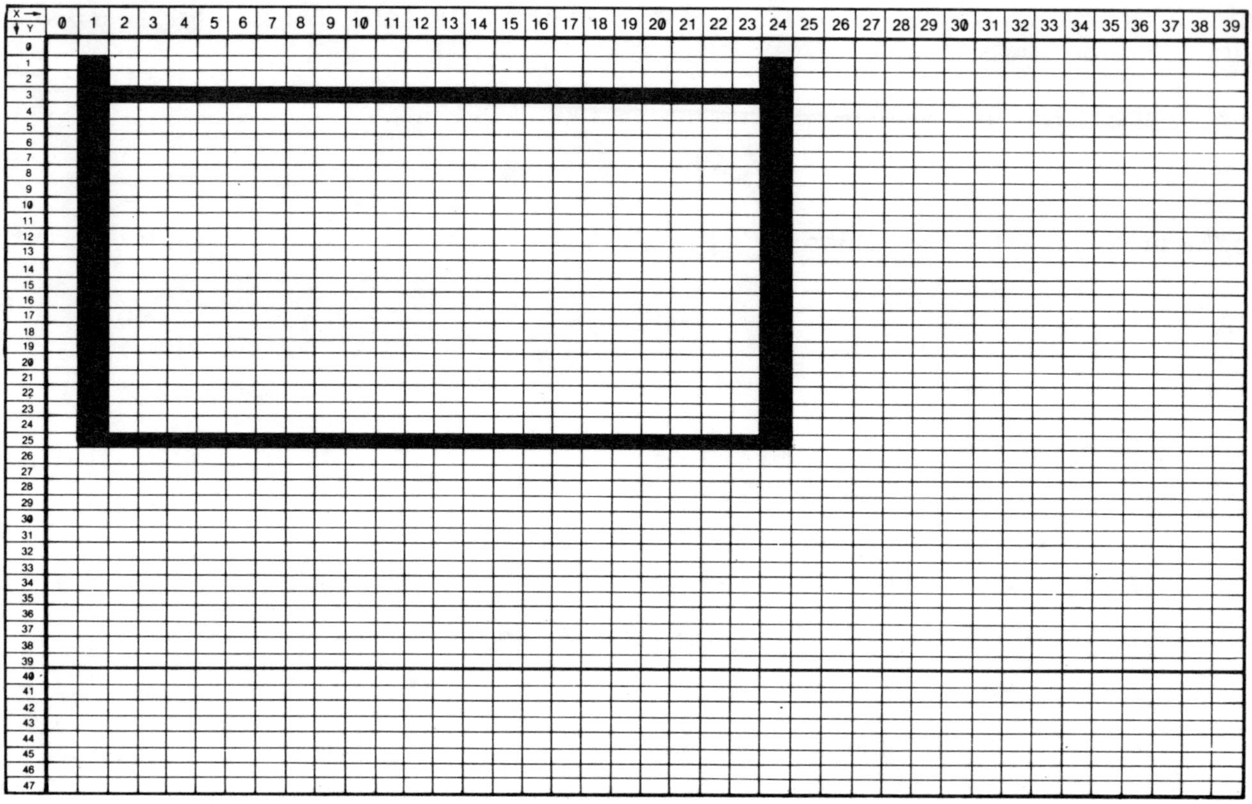

Graphics Letters and Numbers

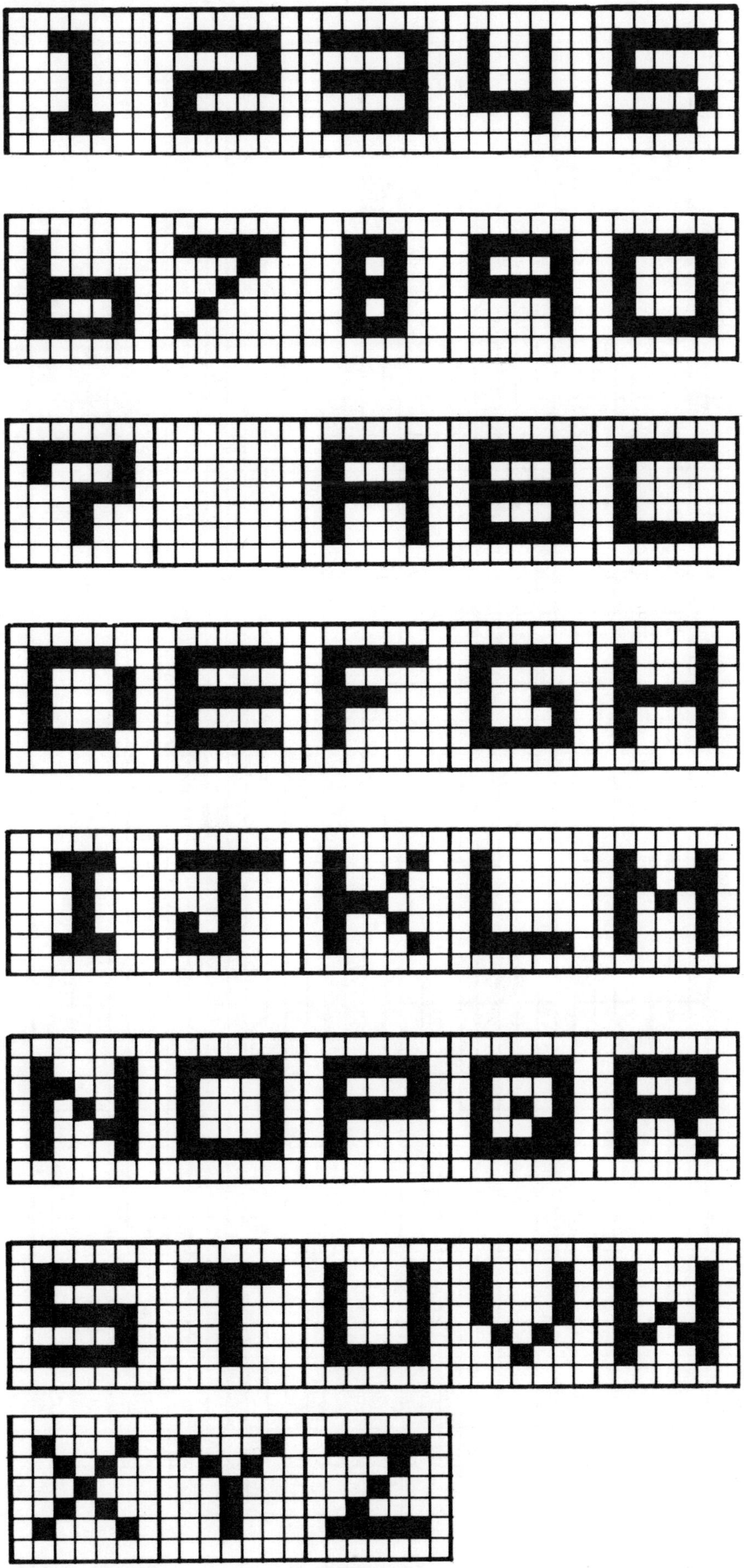

You will need many blank graphic sheets like this.
(use this page for duplication)

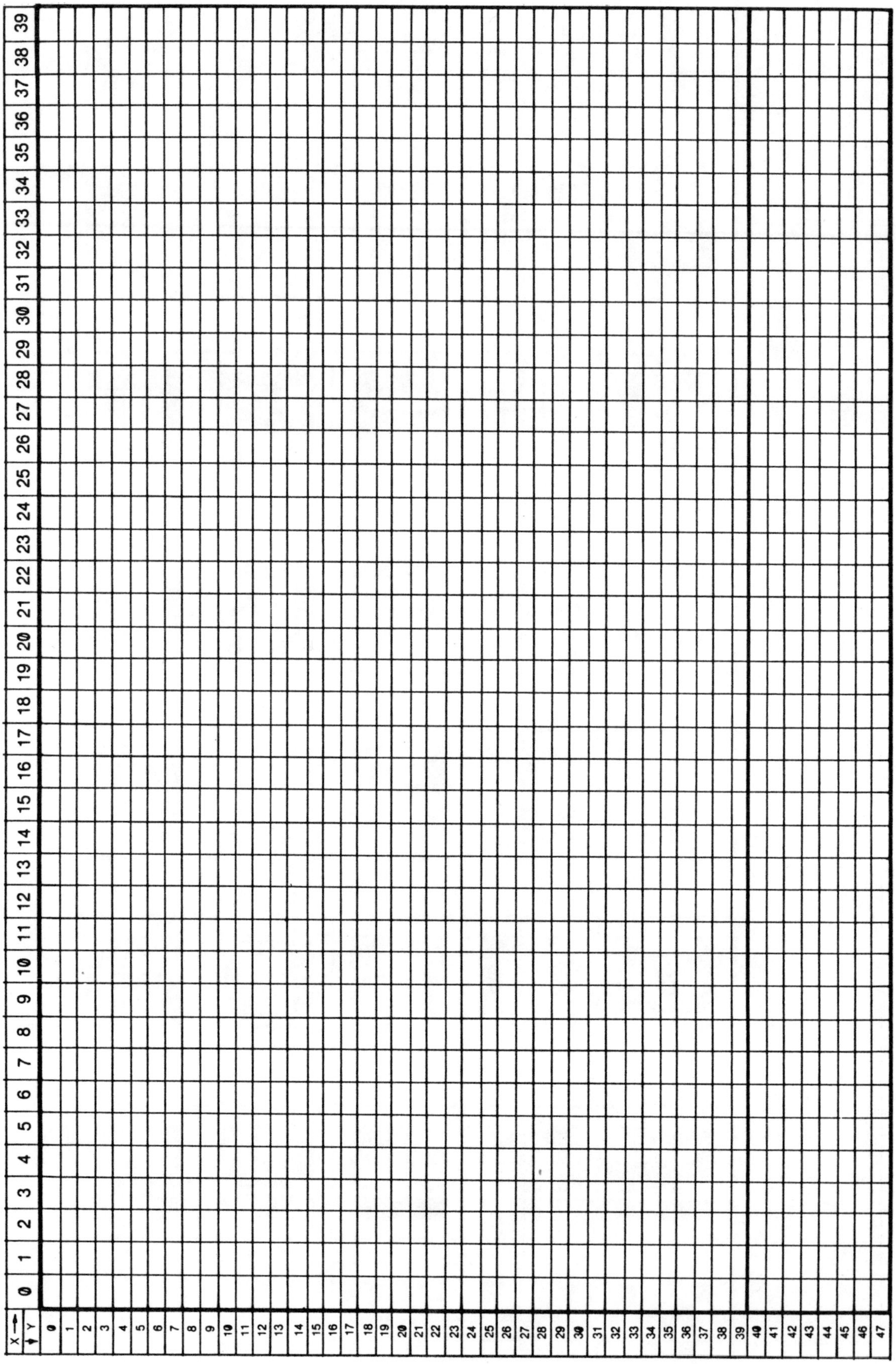

Answer Key to Selected Problems

```
5 HOME
10 REM DRAWS MICRO-MOUSE
20 GR
30 REM ** DRAWS M AND I
40 COLOR = 1
50 HLIN 8,10 AT 6
60 VLIN 2,7 AT 6
70 VLIN 2,7 AT 2
80 PLOT 3,3: PLOT 4,4: PLOT 5,3
90 HLIN 8,10 AT 2
100 VLIN 3,5 AT 9
110 REM ** DRAWS C AND R
120 HLIN 12,14 AT 2
130 HLIN 12,14 AT 6
140 VLIN 3,5 AT 9
150 VLIN 3,5 AT 12
160 VLIN 2,6 AT 16
170 VLIN 2,4 AT 18
180 VLIN 4,5 AT 17
190 PLOT 17,2: PLOT 18,6
200 REM ** DRAWS THE O
210 VLIN 2,6 AT 20
220 VLIN 2,6 AT 22
230 PLOT 21,2: PLOT 21,6
240 REM ** DRAWS THE O AND U
250 VLIN 9,13 AT 3
260 VLIN 9,13 AT 5
270 PLOT 4,9: PLOT 4,13
280 VLIN 15,19 AT 3
290 VLIN 15,19 AT 5
300 PLOT 4,19
310 REM ** DRAWS THE S AND E
320 HLIN 3,5 AT 21
330 HLIN 3,5 AT 23
340 HLIN 3,5 AT 25
350 PLOT 3,22: PLOT 5,24
360 HLIN 3,5 AT 27
370 HLIN 3,5 AT 29
380 HLIN 3,5 AT 31
390 PLOT 3,28: PLOT 3,30
400 REM ** DRAWS HEAD
410 COLOR = 5
420 VLIN 17,21 AT 15
430 VLIN 17,21 AT 16
440 VLIN 17,21 AT 17
450 VLIN 17,21 AT 18
460 VLIN 17,21 AT 19
470 REM ** DRAWS EARS
480 VLIN 12,16 AT 13
490 VLIN 12,16 AT 14
500 VLIN 12,16 AT 15
510 VLIN 12,16 AT 19
520 VLIN 12,16 AT 20
530 VLIN 12,16 AT 21
540 REM ** DRAWS PINK IN EARS
550 COLOR = 11
560 VLIN 13,15 AT 20
570 VLIN 13,15 AT 14
580 REM ** DRAWS NOSE
590 COLOR = 8
600 PLOT 17,19
610 REM ** DRAWS ARMS
620 VLIN 25,28 AT 14
630 VLIN 25,28 AT 20
640 REM **  DRAWS EYES
650 COLOR = 15
660 PLOT 16,18: PLOT 18,18
670 REM ** DRAWS MOUTH
680 COLOR = 1
690 PLOT 17,21
700 REM ** DRAWS CENTER TORSO
710 COLOR = 5
720 VLIN 23,29 AT 16
730 VLIN 23,29 AT 17
740 VLIN 23,29 AT 18
750 REM ** DRAWS RIGHT AND LEFT LEG
760 VLIN 29,34 AT 15
770 VLIN 29,34 AT 19
780 PLOT 15,24: PLOT 19,24
790 PLOT 14,34: PLOT 20,34
800 REM ** DRAWS NECK
810 PLOT 17,22
820 REM ** DRAWS THE TAIL
830 PLOT 19,27: PLOT 21,26
840 PLOT 22,25: PLOT 23,26
850 END
```

```
5 HOME
10 REM DRAWS A FLAG
20 GR
30 REM SCREEN WASH TO WHITE
40 COLOR = 15
50 FOR B = 0 TO 37
60 HLIN 0,39 AT B
70 NEXT B
80 REM DRAWS BLUE STRIPES
90 FOR S = 0 TO 35 STEP 5
100 COLOR = 2
110 HLIN 0,39 AT S
120 HLIN 0,39 AT S + 1
130 HLIN 0,39 AT S + 2
140 NEXT S
150 REM DRAWS RED BACKGROUND
160 COLOR = 1
170 FOR F = 8 TO 29
180 HLIN 10,29 AT F
190 NEXT F
200 REM DRAWS HORIZONTAL WHITE
    LINES ON RED BACKGROUND
210 COLOR = 15
220 FOR S = 11 TO 26 STEP 3
230 HLIN 12,27 AT S
240 NEXT S
250 REM DRAWS VERTICAL LINES
    ON RED TO MAKE SQUARES
260 COLOR = 15
270 FOR S = 12 TO 27 STEP 3
280 VLIN 11,26 AT S
290 NEXT S
300 REM DRAWS BLUE CROSS IN
    CENTER OF RED BACKGROUND
310 COLOR = 2
320 VLIN 15,22 AT 19
330 VLIN 15,22 AT 20
340 HLIN 16,23 AT 18
350 HLIN 16,23 AT 19
360 END
```

```
5 HOME
10 REM TRAFFIC CONTROL SIGNAL
20 GR
30 COLOR = 4
40 FOR X = 6 TO 33
50 HLIN 14,22 AT X
60 NEXT X
70 COLOR = 12
80 FOR X = 25 TO 30
90 HLIN 16,20 AT X
100 NEXT X
110 FOR P = 1 TO 2000: NEXT P
120 COLOR = 5
130 FOR X = 25 TO 30
140 HLIN 16,20 AT X
150 NEXT X
160 COLOR = 13
170 FOR X = 17 TO 22
180 HLIN 16,20 AT X
190 NEXT X
200 FOR P = 1 TO 1000: NEXT P
210 COLOR = 5
220 FOR X = 17 TO 22
230 HLIN 16,20 AT X
240 NEXT X
250 COLOR = 1
260 FOR X = 9 TO 14
270 HLIN 16,20 AT X
280 NEXT X
290 END
```

```
5 HOME
10 REM PROGRAM TO DRAW X ACROSS SCREEN
20 GR
30 Y = 0
40 COLOR = 15
50 FOR X = 0 TO 39
60 PLOT X,Y
70 Y = Y + 1
80 NEXT X
90 Y = 0
100 FOR X = 39 TO 0 STEP -1
110 PLOT X,Y
120 Y = Y + 1
130 NEXT X
140 END
```

```
5 HOME
10 REM VOLCANO ERUPTING
20 GR
30 COLOR = 8
40 REM DRAWS MOUNTAIN
50 HLIN 0,39 AT 39: HLIN 7,31 AT 38
60 HLIN 9,29 AT 37: HLIN 9,29 AT 36
70 HLIN 10,28 AT 35: HLIN 11,27 AT 34
80 HLIN 12,26 AT 33: HLIN 12,26 AT 32
90 HLIN 13,25 AT 31: HLIN 13,25 AT 30
100 HLIN 14,24 AT 29: HLIN 14,24 AT 28
110 HLIN 15,23 AT 27: HLIN 15,23 AT 26
120 HLIN 16,22 AT 25
130 PLOT 17,24: PLOT 21,24
140 REM BEGINNING OF ERUPTION
150 COLOR = 9
160 FOR X = 25 TO 17 STEP -1
170 GOSUB 510
180 HLIN 18,20 AT X
190 NEXT X
200 HLIN 17,21 AT 21: HLIN 17,21 AT 20
210 HLIN 16,22 AT 19: PLOT 15,20
220 PLOT 23,20
230 HLIN 14,24 AT 19: HLIN 15,23 AT 18
240 HLIN 16,22 AT 17: HLIN 17,21 AT 16
250 PLOT 19,15
260 COLOR = 1
265 GOSUB 510
270 HLIN 22,26 AT 17: HLIN 12,16 AT 16
280 HLIN 11,17 AT 17: HLIN 21,27 AT 16
290 HLIN 20,33 AT 15: HLIN 5,18 AT 15
300 HLIN 6,32 AT 14: HLIN 7,31 AT 13
310 HLIN 8,30 AT 12: HLIN 8,30 AT 11
320 HLIN 9,29 AT 10: HLIN 9,29 AT 9
330 HLIN 10,29 AT 8: HLIN 10,28 AT 7
340 HLIN 11,27 AT 6: HLIN 12,16 AT 5
350 HLIN 22,26 AT 5: HLIN 12,15 AT 4
360 HLIN 23,26 AT 4: HLIN 13,14 AT 3
370 HLIN 24,25 AT 3
380 HLIN 5,14 AT 16: HLIN 5,12 AT 17
390 COLOR = 5
400 GOSUB 510
410 HLIN 27,34 AT 16: HLIN 26,34 AT 17
420 HLIN 6,13 AT 18: HLIN 27,34 AT 18
430 HLIN 7,12 AT 19: HLIN 28,33 AT 19
440 HLIN 8,11 AT 20: HLIN 29,32 AT 20
450 PLOT 9,21: GOSUB 530
460 PLOT 10,21: GOSUB 530
470 PLOT 30,21: GOSUB 530
480 PLOT 13,19: GOSUB 530
490 PLOT 25,19
495 GOTO 450
500 REM DELAY ROUTINE
510 FOR P = 1 TO 200: NEXT P
520 RETURN
530 C = INT (14 * RND (1)) + 1
540 COLOR = C
550 RETURN
560 REM PRESS <CONTROL> <C> TO END PROGRAM
```

```
5 HOME
10 REM FISH IN AQUARIUM
20 GR
30 COLOR = 10
40 VLIN 1,25 AT 1: VLIN 1,25 AT 24
50 HLIN 2,23 AT 25
60 REM ADDING THE WATER
70 COLOR = 6
80 FOR X = 3 TO 24
90 HLIN 2,23 AT X
100 NEXT X
110 REM MOVES THE GOLDFISH
120 X = 5:Y = 5
130 READ X$,N,Y$
140 IF Y$ = "Z" THEN END
150 FOR Z = 1 TO N
160 GOSUB 240
170 COLOR = 9
180 PLOT X,Y
190 FOR P = 1 TO 75 : NEXT P
200 COLOR = 6
210 PLOT X,Y
220 NEXT Z
230 GOTO 130
240 IF X$ = "L" THEN X = X - 1
250 IF X$ = "R" THEN X = X + 1
260 IF Y$ = "U" THEN Y = Y - 1
270 IF Y$ = "D" THEN Y = Y + 1
280 IF X$ = "S" THEN X = X
290 IF Y$ = "S" THEN Y = Y
300 RETURN
310 DATA R,10,S, L,5,D
320 DATA S,4,D, R,8,U
330 DATA L,10,S, S,5,D
340 DATA R,8,S, 0,0,Z
400 END
```

Glossary of Terms

COLOR =	A command that sets the color to be drawn on the video screen.
GR	A command that puts the computer in graphics mode.
HLIN	A command that draws a horizontal line.
VLIN	A command that draws a vertical line.
PLOT	A command that draws one cell of color.
TEXT	A command to change the video screen to text mode.
loop	A group of computer commands in a program that perform some action over and over.
cell	A block of color displayed on the video screen.
flag	A letter or number which is used in READ/DATA statements to avoid OUT OF DATA ERROR.
delay loop	A FOR-NEXT loop which creates a pause in a program.
variable	An expression whose value can vary.
GOSUB	A command that sends a computer to a subroutine in a program.
RETURN	A command that sends the computer back to the next BASIC statement in the main program.
READ/DATA	Two BASIC commands that give values to numeric or string variables. READ assigns the values. DATA holds the values to be read.
x-axis	A line that runs left to right on a video screen.
y-axis	A line that runs from the top to the bottom of a video screen.